HEROES IN OUR MIDST

*Top Canadian Athletes Share Personal Stories
from Their Lives in Sport*

Edited by Robin Mednick and Wendy Thomas

M&S

National Library of Canada Cataloguing in Publication Data

Heroes in our midst : top Canadian athletes share personal stories from their lives in sport / edited by Robin Mednick and Wendy Thomas.

ISBN 0-7710-5681-8 (bound).–ISBN 0-7710-5682-6 (pbk.)

1. Athletes–Canada–Biography. I. Thomas, Wendy, 1942- II. Mednick, Robin, 1953- III. Title.

GV697.A1H47 2001   796'.092'271   C2001-900875-9

We acknowledge the financial support of the Government of Canada through the Book Publishing Industry Development Program for our publishing activities. We further acknowledge the support of the Canada Council for the Arts and the Ontario Arts Council for our publishing program.

Design: Terri-Anne Fong
Typeset in Bembo by M&S, Toronto

Printed and bound in Canada

This book is printed on acid-free paper that is 100% ancient-forest friendly (100% post-consumer recycled).

McClelland & Stewart Ltd.
The Canadian Publishers
481 University Avenue
Toronto, Ontario
M5G 2E9
www.mcclelland.com

1 2 3 4 5   06 05 04 03 02

CONT

Foreword

Introduction

1. The Way We Were
2. Little Moments, Big Lessons
3. The Pain of It All
4. Opportunity Knocks
5. Beyond the Barriers
6. The Price of Fame
7. I Owe It All To . . .
8. Unforgettable
9. Why Not Me?   99
10. Get Back on the Horse   115
11. Unexpected Heroes   128
12. Oh No!   137
13. Tough Choices   149
14. Let the Games Begin   158
15. We Are Family   172
16. At the Heart of It   189
17. A Child's Gift   208
18. So Proud! So Proud!   221

Acknowledgements   236
Index of Contributors   240

FOREWORD

In 1998 I had the great honour of being part of the hockey team that represented Canada at the Olympic Winter Games in Nagano, Japan. I had dreamed of being part of the Olympic Games for many years, so it was a thrill to be able to accept when the opportunity presented itself!

One of the highlights of being in Nagano was the time our team spent living in the Olympic Village. We saw up close the dedication, commitment, agony, and joy that are part of any sport. We were able to share with these talented amateur athletes their highs and lows and our own highs and lows. All of us on the team recognized the emotions known to all athletes – whether they're on a hometown swimming team or competing to be considered the best curlers in the world. People who strive for excellence, whether on or off the sports field – or hockey rink! – identify with the satisfaction of a job well done or the disappointment in not reaching goals.

But few people know the struggles that athletes face behind the scenes – struggles that take them to the limits of their endurance and help them to reach their full potential. In *Heroes in Our Midst*, you'll get a glimpse of what goes on, both in private and in public, as athletes strive to reach continually challenging goals in an attempt to conquer their fears, setbacks, and physical limitations. These remarkable personal accounts from Canadian athletes, including Olympians and Paralympians, help explain the courage and dedication that drive them to continue, sometimes in the face of truly daunting odds. It's because of those daunting odds that I am pleased that the proceeds from the sale of this book will go to the Foundation for Athletes and Sport Training (FAST), a charitable organization created by the Toronto 2008 Olympic Bid to benefit junior developing athletes and education in sport throughout Canada.

Reading these stories brought back my memories of Nagano. My time there confirmed something I'd known from my life in professional sport: winning isn't always about getting the gold. Sometimes it's about doing the best you can, sometimes it's about taking defeat and learning from it. Not only did I see this over and over at those Olympic Games, I see it in these stories of dreams and personal triumphs. I hope you enjoy reading these stories and that they inspire you in your own life.

Wayne Gretzky

INTRODUCTION

I

It started as a gift for my son Zale's bar mitzvah, a coming-of-age ritual in the Jewish tradition. What wise words could I impart to my youngest, to welcome him into the adult world?

I had plenty of time to think about this on the plane to the Olympic Games in Sydney, Australia. I went as the Co-ordinator for a team of 25 Canadian athletes who were there to represent Toronto's 2008 Olympic Bid.

Working with the Bid for three years, I had come to know and respect these incredible athletes. Perhaps life's lessons through their eyes would be instructive to my son. I asked the athletes to write him letters, sharing what they had learned from their life experiences. Some joined together to write inspiring words. Others gave personal gems from their own sporting lives. It was a collection of humorous, heartwarming, and wise advice.

Then it hit me. Why stop there? Why should my son be the only one to benefit from the athletes' words of wisdom? Why couldn't we share these poignant stories with the rest of Canada and the world?

David Crombie, Chair of the Bid, John Bitove, President and CEO, and the Toronto Olympic Bid staff wholeheartedly agreed. This was a Bid "by athletes, for athletes" and the book would be a true reflection of this commitment. To my delight, McClelland & Stewart enthusiastically endorsed the project. All we needed were the stories!

Athletes across the country, from grass roots to Olympians and Paralympians, were approached. We wanted their memorable moments – ones that made them laugh or cry; ones that made an impact on their lives; moments that forever changed how they viewed themselves and the world around them.

Within a single month, more than 160 athletes answered the call – many more than could be included in one volume. They wrote from their hearts: stories of humanity and generosity; stories of hard work and dedication; stories from young and old, with the perspective of youth and the wisdom of age. Each story feels like an intimate conversation conveyed with vivid detail and genuine warmth.

I have such high regard for the Canadian athletes I have met. They have taught me that accomplishment in sport is not about medals but about achieving personal excellence. Sport is not about money or fame. It is about lifelong friendships and the pursuit of dreams. Most of all, these amazing athletes have taught me the true meaning of modesty and humility.

I dedicate the effort and passion that went into the creation of this book to Canadian athletes everywhere – past, present, and future.

They are quite simply heroes in our midst.

Robin Mednick

Books take on a life of their own in the manuscript stage – they can be unruly and difficult to discipline; they can be a bit unfocused; sometimes they're charming but slight or overly ponderous. Then there are those rare times that a manuscript comes together, like this one did, in a magical act of creation. It's the equivalent, I think, to what athletes call "being in the zone." The zone is that point when all the training and discipline result in a performance that's effortless, enjoyable, and outstanding. It's when everything works. This book is a clear indication that athletes can be in the zone on the page as well as on the track, in the pool, on horseback, or on wheels, whether wheelchair or bicycle.

As if it was meant to be, we got stories from all age ranges – from James Worrall and Hilda Young, both athletes in the Olympic Games in Berlin, 1936, to Alexandre Despatie, a youthful 15, and Moorea Longstaff, now 18, with a piece she wrote when she was 13. We got stories of unforgettable world events, with Robert Finlay and Paul Henderson recalling the tragedy in 1972 at Munich, and Dan Thompson's memories of the boycott of the 1980 Games in Moscow. And we got the personal – Sandra McCaig talking about her family of competitive windsurfers, Patrick Jarvis telling how his brothers coached him in catching a ball after his disabling childhood accident, Marnie McBean taking us through the agony, both physical and emotional, of injury.

Stories came in from people who've competed at everything from the local level to the Olympics and Paralympics. Some of these athletes came home with medals, some without – Bruce Kidd, who movingly writes of his appearance at the 1964 Olympic Games in Tokyo, "I am still haunted by those failures"; Jeff Adams, who had to cope with an unusual mechanical failure; Daniel Igali, who talks about the dreams that motivate. Other athletes share with us tales from national and world championships and Commonwealth and Pan American Games – Jennifer Robinson's serendipitous discovery that there was a positive side to injury; Monique Kavelaars's concern for another athlete; and Robert Iarusci's snapshot of the great Pelé.

Without asking, we got stories that covered the spectrum of amateur sports – among them wrestling, boxing, sailing, canoeing, wheelchair racing, triathlon, beach volleyball, baseball, speed skating, synchronized swimming, diving, hockey, water polo, weightlifting, aerial freestyle skiing. Even the sport of luge is represented in Chris Wightman's beautiful piece that is part eulogy to Sarajevo and part description of the thrill and terror of hurtling down a narrow icy passage.

A book like this would not be complete without humour to balance the tales of disappointment, injury, and pain – can there be any more vivid example of the way athletes push themselves than Kristina Groves's wry description of how her body reacts after a gruelling speed skating race? For the lighter side of sport, seek out an unusual cure for a sore finger in Akos Sandor's tale or find out why Sylvie Bernier stopped chewing gum. James Ransom tells his story of a volunteer bus driver in a lighthearted fashion, although the outcome was less than amusing for him. Finally, find out in Dave O'Donnell's story why you don't want to be a fly on the floor when a crackerjack fencer is nearby.

As we reviewed the many stories that athletes sent in, common themes emerged – the power of a dream, coping with failure, the importance of small gestures, the drive to improve, the importance of having fun – and the stories in these pages are representative of them all. But another theme was apparent – these are Canadian stories, even when played out on an international stage. The fundamental decency of Canadians, their thoughtfulness, shines through time after time – Peter Fonseca jeopardizing his race to do a favour for a friend, athletes giving up their spots on Olympic teams for a teammate, Hayley Wickenheiser, the youngest on her team, leaving a note of encouragement for France St-Louis, the oldest. Their pride in being Canadian is well demonstrated in descriptions of the Opening Ceremonies of various Olympic and Pan American Games – with some humour thrown in, of course. But what better illustrates the image Canadians have of themselves – modest people who quietly do the right thing – than Margie Schuett's story, which ends this book?

And now these stories are ready for you, the reader. You don't need to be a sports fan or an athlete to enjoy them – these tales transcend sport. They speak to anyone who has had a dream, who has been in a competition (remember that footrace at your father's company's picnic?), who has put themselves on the line to be the best they can be. In these wonderful stories you'll find solace, hope, entertainment, and inspiration – and you'll also share in the joy of being in the zone.

Wendy Thomas

• 1 •

THE WAY WE WERE

The 1932 Olympic Games in Los Angeles were the first ones where movie stars attended in great numbers to see the athletes perform. One day there was a lull in the Games so the athletes went over to the "stars" to get their autographs. These celebrities were particularly interested in the fact that we were from Canada – they wanted autographs from as many athletes outside the United States as possible. So there we were, getting autographs from people like Gary Cooper, and they were getting autographs from a bunch of runners from Canada!

This fleeting fame didn't last long. Our 4 × 400-metre relay team had won the bronze medal in a race in which all three medal-winning teams had broken the Olympic record, but when I got home, I couldn't get a job anywhere – no one wanted to hire someone who was black. There weren't really such things as endorsements or speaking tours to help you earn money then. People kept saying, "Have you tried the railroad?" So I finally did. There was no other place to work.

I worked on the railroad for 22 years – years that were difficult and humiliating but which taught me great lessons about people and life.

– Ray Lewis, Olympic bronze medallist, Track and Field, Olympic Games, Los Angeles, 1932

JAMES WORRALL

Sixty-five years have passed since I laced up my new, ill-fitting track shoes and dug my own starting holes in the track at Berlin's Olympic Stadium. I was competing in the 110-metre hurdles race and the 400-metre hurdles. Much has changed in the lives of modern Olympic track athletes since that time. They wear shoes that fit properly and benefit from the use of state-of-the-art starting blocks and timing systems; they fly around the world in airplanes. However, I think that we may have had the best of it when we travelled by sea and by train to get to Berlin in 1936. During our week on the Atlantic in that much more leisurely era, lifelong friendships blossomed. And it was the entire team together – 110 athletes and 30 officials – not just us track athletes on our own. Being well over six feet tall, I confess I did find the bunks on the *Duchess of Bedford* rather cramped, but the ship was large enough that we did laps on the decks to try to keep in shape. The boxers even set up an impromptu ring on one of the ship's hatch covers. I played deck tennis and won my first Olympic "trophy," a *Duchess of Bedford* beer stein.

On board with us were a thousand or so of Canada's First World War veterans en route to the dedication of the Canadian memorial at Vimy Ridge in France. They took a great interest in us, the new generation going to Europe to represent Canada – with the significant difference that ours was to be a peaceful competition.

We landed in Le Havre and boarded a train for Paris where we were treated to lunch in a large *brasserie* followed by a bus tour of the city. After a 20-hour overnight train trip to Berlin, sitting or sleeping uncomfortably on our luggage, we received a red-carpet reception at the Friedrichsstrasse station, complete with a band playing "The Maple Leaf Forever," a tune to which few of us knew the words.

The first Olympic Village had been created for the Games of 1932 in Los Angeles, and the Germans improved on the concept. Their village was in a 325-acre park, with woods, fine lawns, a small lake, and excellent training facilities. In the recreation hall, I saw television for the first time – a basic closed-circuit system allowing us to view events taking place in the stadium. None of us could imagine the impact this new technology was going to have on the Olympic Games of the future.

A day or so before the Opening Ceremonies, Sam Manson, our General Manager, called me into his office and told me I had been selected flag-bearer for our team. I was a very excited young man. I am sure I share with all flag-bearers the memory of what a thrill it is to enter the vast stadium and hear the cheers of the thousands of spectators in the stands. In retrospect, I experienced a unique moment in world history. As we lined up before the ceremony, on the Maifeld adjacent to the Olympic Stadium, I stood with the Red Ensign on a flagpole, at attention, as the political leaders of Germany paraded by a few metres from me. Heading into the stadium along with International Olympic Committee president Count Baillet-Latour was Adolf Hitler, together with Goering, Goebbels, and other high-ranking Nazis. The menace these men represented was not yet apparent – the Second World War was still three long years in the future.

Although it was my fate not to win any Olympic medals in 1936, I feel that I have been an Olympic winner, nonetheless, through my lifelong involvement with athletes, sport, and the ideals of the Olympic movement. Berlin was the beginning.

JAMES WORRALL was a member of the Canadian Olympic Team in Track and Field at the Olympic Games in Berlin, 1936. He was Chef de Mission for the Canadian Olympic Team in Melbourne, 1956, and Rome, 1960. He was President of the Canadian Olympic Association (COA) from 1961 to 1967 and is now honorary Life President. He was also a member of the International Olympic Committee (IOC) from 1967 to 1989 and remains an honorary member. He is an officer of the Order of Canada.

HILDA YOUNG

In 1936, training for the Olympics was so different than now. We didn't have any financial help. We had track practice a couple of times a week, and because there were no facilities in the winter for training, we didn't train at all until the warmer weather allowed outdoor practice. Sometimes a factory would allow us space to run during the winter, but this was rare.

When we arrived in Berlin for the 1936 Olympics, each Canadian athlete was given a red blazer and a tracksuit, but we had to buy our own dresses and shoes. They had to be white dresses, and the men wore white pants and shirts. We marched into the stadium for the Opening Ceremonies in strict formation, not strolling in as they do in modern times. This was also the first Olympics where pigeons were released into the sky. Hitler was in the stands every day and the people would cheer for a half-hour at a time. We didn't know then what we do today.

HILDA YOUNG was a bronze medallist in the 4 × 100-metre relay in Track and Field at the Olympic Games in Berlin, 1936.

BRUCE KIDD

The Olympics have broadened my horizons ever since I first heard about them from my father in 1952. That summer, he was about to depart for a conference in Denmark, when a friend at the CBC asked him if, if they gave him a camera and showed him how to use it, he would film the Olympics in nearby Finland for the new national television network that was to be launched later that year. My father had worshipped Percy Williams as a boy growing up in Vancouver and had followed the Olympics all his life. He jumped at the opportunity. He was the entire CBC TV crew in Helsinki – writer, director, producer, cameraperson, and commentator.

On his return to Toronto, he showed every foot of the 15 hours of film he took to his nine-year-old son. That footage, the stories he brought back about the great athletes from all over the world, and the spirit of internationalism he described throughout the Games made me realize that sports we rarely heard of in Canada were played at a very high level elsewhere, and that the Olympics were bigger and more exciting than anything I had ever imagined. I vowed that I would get there myself some day.

I got my own chance to explore the world through Olympic sport a few years later when I joined the East York Track Club (EYTC). I'm not sure whether I would have pursued long-distance running if I had not known it was in the Olympics. But I quickly discovered that it gave me an enormous sense of pleasure and discovery. There is nothing more satisfying than getting into a rhythm, running quickly but under control kilometre after kilometre, and then throwing in a burst of speed — whether it was to break or overtake someone in a race, or for the joy of flying on a private run. I loved to run anywhere, indoors or out, on the track or road, even up hills. I still get the urge to run when I approach a large hill. It was immensely satisfying to cover large distances under your own power. I discovered large sectors of Toronto and other cities on training runs.

Under coach Fred Foot, the EYTC had sent a steady stream of athletes to the Olympics and other major international games. At a time when the schools I attended seemed to stifle ambition in the interests of conservative conformity, Fred challenged us to think about racing against — and beating — the rest of the world. It was a heady atmosphere. It was not very long before I was winning major championships, breaking

records, and receiving invitations to race in the great cities of
the world. In the waning days of amateurism, travel was considered one of the great rewards of athleticism, and we were
encouraged to explore the culture and politics of the countries
we visited. My teammates and I made the most of it. It was a
privileged introduction to the rich diversity of humankind.

When I actually reached the Olympics in Tokyo in 1964,
my races were disappointing. Injured, I ran anyway and fared
poorly. I am still haunted by those failures. But the Games
provided other affirmation. Other athletes performed magni-
ficently, and it was strangely comforting to be a witness to
such accomplishment. Tokyo marked my first visit to a non-
European culture, and it was full of eye-opening adventures.
My favourite was the fish market, where thousands of species,
many of which I had never heard of, were docked, auctioned,
cleaned, consumed, and sold in a vast area entirely devoted to
fish. After our events were over, Abby Hoffman and I travelled
throughout Japan on our own. We were knocked out by
Japanese achievement, culture, and hospitality. I went to
Hiroshima on my own – the final torch-bearer for the Games
was born on the morning the atom bomb had been dropped
on Hiroshima – and was deeply moved by the number of
people, who could speak no other English, who approached
me to say, "No more Hiroshima!" It demonstrated how the
Olympics could open communication across the divides of
culture, tap into the great creativity of different peoples, and
give voice to their great longing for peace. It whetted my
appetite for further travel and intercultural exploration, and
made me a lifelong advocate of the Olympic movement.

There are other windows on the world. But for those of us
who love sports, there is nothing like the Olympic movement

to throw us into the rich complexity and diversity of the world, to provide the stimulus and delight of a world community. I've attended four other Olympic Games, and countless other Olympic-related events around the world, and I have learned from and been stretched intellectually and emotionally by every one of them. The contribution of the Olympic movement goes well beyond the inspirational feats of the athletes it encourages. The stimulus and opportunity it provides for international communication, emulation, and exchange is an enormous force for the advancement of human societies.

BRUCE KIDD was a long-distance runner who represented Canada at the Olympic Games in Tokyo, 1964. He was the gold medallist at the Commonwealth Games at Perth, 1962, and was Canada's Athlete of the Year in 1961 and 1962.

REG McCLELLAN

In 1975, I was part of the Canadian Wheelchair Basketball Team. Within a six-week period our team travelled to Aylesbury, England, for the World Multi-Sport Games, to Bruges, Belgium, for the first World Championships for Wheelchair Basketball and then directly to Mexico City, Mexico, for the Pan American Games.

These are some of the thoughts and feelings extracted from my writings 25 years ago:

Flying as a team, so far
from west to east and then overseas

no onboard chair, don't drink
arrive excited, dehydrated
we need to change this.

Stoke Mandeville in the summer
wet, cold, drab
barracks are home, airplane hangars
sliding doors with a wingspan plus
86 beds
one bathtub
six toilets in the open
lots of onionskin toilet paper
wipe or scrape
read or write on it
onionskin talk throughout the team.
TV dinners, night beer tent with fish and chips
outdoor practice court, no hoops
in England, lost, alone, then we compete.

Competition, ready
full gymnasium, intimate and loud
we lose by 65, 55, and 45 in first three games.

Bruges, different . . . not
tuxedos, seven-course meal
gymnasium great
tents with army cots
outdoor drive-through shower
outdoor flush toilets
U.S.A. leaves infested indoor facilities
we debug their digs.

Competition, ready
full gymnasium, intimate and loud
I pass to Walter for two at the buzzer
we win and get out of the "B" division.

Mexico, no chairs for three days
airline sorry
beans every day
sewer back up daily
pink stoppers, Pepto-Bismol and any liquid.

Competition, ready
full gymnasium, intimate and loud
we gel as a team
finish strong.

Always the same
deplorable conditions
games start and

Hot blood
trickling through tiny tunnels
as the earth runs fast for the floor.

A crying crowd
claps
as friendship
reigns o'er competition!

Canada is number one today
for juniors,

for women,
and for men!

REG McCLELLAN has specialized in Wheelchair Basketball and has participated at every level in the sport over the last three decades. He has received honours and awards as a player, coach, volunteer, and administrator. He is an executive member of the International Wheelchair Basketball Federation.

• 2 •

LITTLE MOMENTS,
BIG LESSONS

I remember watching Canadian boxers Willie de Wit and Shawn O'Sullivan accept their medals at the 1984 Olympic Games in Los Angeles. I'll never forget the pride on their faces. Although I was inspired and determined to succeed, I wondered if it would ever be possible to be an Olympian; would I be able to train that hard; would I ever be that good; would I be able to compete with the best in the world?

– Michael Strange, member of Canada's Boxing Team, Olympic Games, Barcelona, 1992, Atlanta, 1996, Sydney, 2000

CURT HARNETT

In the summer of 1996, as the Atlanta Olympics fast approached, I was considered one of the gold medal favourites in my event, men's match sprint (cycling). After my silver medal performance at the 1995 World Championships, breaking and retaining the world record, and my previous Olympic experience (three Olympics, two medals), I admit that I had some pretty high expectations for myself and believed that the gold medal was well within my reach.

But, on July 27, 1996, the same day someone set off a bomb at the Centennial Olympic Park in downtown Atlanta, my dreams of completing my Olympic medal collection – I already had a silver and a bronze – were dashed. In my semifinal matchup, American Marty Nothstein defeated me in two straight rides and advanced to the gold medal match.

My loss relegated me to race for third or fourth place, matched up against the rider who was defeated in the other semifinal matchup, Gary Niewand of Australia. Gary was a longtime rival, training partner, and friend. This race was to occur the next day.

The thought of coming away from the Atlanta Olympics

without a medal had never entered my mind as I prepared for competition. All my mental imagery had me on the Olympic podium, proudly displaying my medal. Now, the opposite was a potential reality, as my final match for the bronze would be no walk in the park. In recent major events, Gary had had the better of me.

Due to our relationship, Gary and I had discussed how remarkable it would be for us to race each other in the final for the gold medal. He was the only rider in the field I would ever accept losing to. I admired his abilities on and off the bicycle.

The drive back to the village from the track usually took 45 minutes. But on this day, it seemed to take a minute and forever, both at the same time.

I was doing some serious and intense soul-searching. What was I in this for? What was it all about? Why am I here? What is left?

Eventually, I arrived at the village, still with no answers. My dreams had been dashed – or so I thought. I made it to my room in the athletes' village and sat on the edge of my bed. I felt all alone. I had to get myself something to eat, I had to get some therapy for my leg, and I had to prepare for tomorrow.

But I remember asking myself, "Why bother?"

I did what I had to – ate, got my leg attended to – but mechanically, without much thought. I was in a daze. I was still searching for something, searching for an answer. My attitude was not that of champion, as doubt was leading me down the wrong path.

I made it to dinner. I don't remember what I ate, or with whom. I got some more therapy on my leg. I made it back to my room. I prepared my track bag for the next day – still in a daze.

It was then that one particular memory passed through my mind.

When the event I was recalling happened, its effect on me didn't seem anything out of the ordinary. But, as I was soon to discover, its impact was profound.

My preparation for the '96 Games took place in Minneapolis, Minnesota, because the Velodrome in Minneapolis was very similar to the facility in Atlanta. The beauty of being in Minneapolis was that it was only a five-hour drive from my hometown of Thunder Bay, Ontario. On the weekends, my wife and son would make the drive to Minneapolis to visit with me.

During my daily training sessions at the track, my son Skylar – who at the time was six – would get quite excited watching me go round and round on the track. This was at a time when he was learning to ride his own bike without training wheels.

At the completion of my training sessions and my training day, Skylar would be keen to head out into the parking lot of the hotel to try to get himself up on two wheels without assistance. Methodically, we would make our way from one end to the other. The whole time I was holding Skylar's seat while he repeated, "Dad, don't let go, Dad, don't let go!"

Eventually, I did let go. His voice grew fainter as the distance between us increased, and he covered about 200 metres on his own before he tumbled to the ground. It was the look on his face as he was picking himself up, realizing that he had just covered those last 200 or so metres on his own, that was forever stored in my memory.

It was that smile, that sense of accomplishment, of freedom and of pride that replayed in my mind as I sat on the edge of my bed. It was that expression that best described why I rode my bike in the first place.

That is why I was here, at the Olympics – because I *loved* to ride my bike!

The competition? Why, it was just an excuse, an excuse for me to ride my bike day in and day out. Sure, there were goals and dreams, but they were all channelled through my absolute desire to ride, to ride my bike like the wind.

That next day, July 28, was a day like no other for me. I was going to go out there and have the time of my life. (Heck, it was my parents' 40th wedding anniversary, and although I could have just bought them a new toaster, I was going to get them an Olympic medal!)

I rode the finals against Gary like I had never ridden before. Every pedal stroke, every manoeuvre remains fresh in my mind. I remember that day as if it were only yesterday. And through it all, I did have the time of my life! All my desire, dedication, and determination were there. All my passion and hunger for success were there. As were my smile and excitement. I was humbled by the moment.

I went on to capture the bronze medal that day, in the greatest day of bike racing I ever had! But it was not great because I had just won my third Olympic medal, it was great because I had the most fun a guy could ever have on a bicycle!

It was all because of a lesson that was taught to me by my six-year-old son. Isn't it supposed to be the other way around?

CURT HARNETT won a silver medal in Cycling at the Olympic Games in Los Angeles, 1984, a bronze medal in Barcelona, 1992, and a bronze medal in Atlanta, 1996. He was a member of the Canadian Olympic Team in Seoul, 1988.

TRACEY FERGUSON

As far as I remember, I was always interested in sports. Playing, watching, or talking with friends about some game or race that had happened was the best way to spend my time. It didn't hurt that I had four older brothers and a sister who were active in sport too. Being the youngest, I did everything I could to join in their games. I took their old hockey sticks and cut them down to my size so I was prepared for the nightly game of street hockey. In the summer, I would constantly challenge my friends and siblings to swim races in our pool. I made everything I did into a competition and took them all seriously.

In the spring, just before I turned 10 years old, I was scheduled to have surgery to correct a curvature in my spine. I anticipated being able to compete in school sports in the fall.

When I woke up from the surgery, I was unable to move my legs. I could barely feel anything below my knees and was not even able to sit up. Never mind playing sports, I was just hoping I would be able to walk again. Instead of worrying about my slap-shot or stickhandling, I was taking on a new challenge of physiotherapy. This was some of the most gruelling training I have ever done. Every day I would work on tasks that were once mundane – just trying to straighten my leg or lift it off the ground. With time and a lot of sweat and persistence, I was starting to regain some function in my legs. But it was pretty certain I would not be able to run again. My love of sports had not died but it seemed that my chances of playing them had.

Whenever I was in the pool, though, it did not seem to matter that I didn't have all my leg function. I still loved to swim, and the freedom in the water was amazing. While my kick was not as strong as it once was, my arms were much stronger. I still won most of the races against my friends. I told my parents that I wanted to start swimming on a competitive team. There was one hitch in all this, and that was that I could not dive. Since diving is the way to enter the water and gives swimmers the bulk of their momentum, I would be at a major disadvantage. My mother knew that with my competitive nature I would not enjoy being beaten all the time. So she looked into programs for swimmers with a disability.

We found out about a place called Variety Village, where the sports and training facility is fully accessible and offers opportunities for both able-bodied and disabled. The pool was still in the planning stages, so I put swimming on hold for a while and took on the challenge of wheelchair basketball.

While I never imagined being a wheelchair basketball player when I was younger, the sport seemed to find me and I fell in love with it. The funny thing about basketball was that, as much as I loved playing it, when I first started out, I was terrible. I understood the game and was fast in my wheel-chair but was unable to do one of the most important things in the game: shoot. When you play standing up, most of the power for your shot comes from your legs. But sitting in a wheelchair means that the power is not there. All your strength comes from your arms. So I had a new challenge if I wanted to be successful as a wheelchair basketball player – getting strong enough to shoot a basket. It was three months before I was able to make my first basket, and those months were filled with hours in the park or school gym trying to shoot. At times it was very frustrating. Some days it seemed that I would never make a basket, but I knew that if I gave up trying that

I was certainly never going to make a basket. So with plenty of missed shots, I continued to keep shooting, knowing that one day the ball would go in.

After I made my first basket, it felt like a lid had been lifted off the hoop and the baskets have continued to go in ever since. At the age of 16, I made the Women's National Wheelchair Basketball Team and was the youngest player to do so. I have since competed in three Paralympic Games and two World Championships, winning gold in all of them.

When I was 10, my world changed when I ended up in a wheelchair, but it is something I would never change back. It opened up a world of opportunity for me through wheelchair basketball and the chance to represent Canada. With persistence on the court and off the court, many of my dreams have come true.

TRACEY FERGUSON won three consecutive gold medals for Canada in Women's Wheelchair Basketball at the Paralympic Games in Barcelona, 1992, Atlanta, 1996, and Sydney, 2000. She won the World Championships in 1994 and 1998. In 1998 she was named to the World All-Star Team.

SYLVIE BIGRAS

One of my strongest memories is from the 1998 Olympic Winter Games in Nagano, Japan, where I acted as Press Chief. A young athlete came in to phone his hometown newspaper. He was almost in tears because he had finished around 50th. He was bent over, quiet and clearly ashamed of himself. Without wanting to preach a sermon, I told him to hold his head high and be proud, that not only was he Canada's (an entire nation!) best in his sport, he was an Olympian, and one of the best in the world. Fiftieth – why, we worship NHL players who may be 2000th in the world – everything is relative, isn't it? I told this young athlete that years from now, he would not remember his exact result – he would remember how he felt when he was named to the Olympic Team and what it was like to walk into the Olympic Stadium during Opening Ceremonies. He would remember the people he met, and the butterflies in his stomach when he positioned himself at the starting gate.

It is the journey that matters – how we are transformed by the experience of sport – and how we become better people because of it.

SYLVIE BIGRAS was the assistant Chef de Mission at the Olympic Games in Barcelona, 1992, and press chief of the Canadian Olympic Team at the Olympic Winter Games in Nagano, 1998. She was a member of the University of Ottawa's silver medal team in Volleyball, 1980.

SILKEN LAUMANN

The most important lessons I learned from sport I learned rowing backwards in a wooden boat. These lessons were about how to win and how to lose. In a world of sport that seems to divide itself so clearly into winners and losers, I learned about the role of chance, luck, and fate in winning.

I also questioned the logic that if only one person won the race everybody else was a loser.

If winning is winning the race, I haven't actually won very often. But one of the best winning moments of my career was in 1991 in Vienna at the World Rowing Championships. I was locked in battle with a powerful Romanian sculler, Elisabeta Lipa, for the entire final race. Spectators told me later the lead changed five times and that for the first 1,500 metres of this 2,000-metre race there was never more than a second between us. With 500 metres to go, I made a bid for the lead and she answered my challenge, taking the lead once again. Finally with 30 strokes to go, I took the lead and she couldn't answer. The rower in third place was so far behind that the Romanian eased off, and within a few strokes I had open water. I knew I was going to win. I had the luxury of 30 strokes to enjoy being the best in the world. It was intox-icating. I remember saying to myself, "Enjoy this, it may never happen again."

Losing helps you appreciate winning. In 1995 I had the worst year of my career. I was recovering emotionally from my Benadryl experience, when I had mistakenly taken a cold medication that contained a banned ingredient. The media attention this mistake received made me realize for the first time how much I really was in the public eye. My confidence was shattered, but I fought back. Every race was a struggle. Many times that year I wanted to quit. Rowing wasn't fun anymore. There was too much pressure. I felt I couldn't make another mistake. This thinking paralyzed any great perform-ance I might have had. After the European Championships in Lucerne, where I finished seventh, my coach and I discussed quitting. He presented it as an option and it really scared me. I didn't want to finish my career on this note.

The next six weeks were the most difficult of my career. I struggled to gain back my confidence. One day I would feel great, the next I would be riddled with self-doubts. As I prepared for the final race of the season, I didn't know what the outcome would be. At the World Championships I got into the final by the skin of my teeth. The final was going to be do or die. If I didn't perform to the best of my ability I knew that I would quit the sport. I couldn't have another season like this one.

Rowing up to the starting line, I was extremely nervous. Halfway up to the start, I rowed past the medal presentation dock where the medals for the women's double sculls were being awarded. Kathleen Heddle and Marnie McBean had just won the race and were rowing away from the dock with a gold medal. Marnie yelled out in an enthusiastic voice, "Go for it, Silken, you're good." Her words encouraged me so much. The double from the Netherlands had won the silver medal, and Irene – who I had raced against for years in the single sculls – cheered me on too. Philippa Baker in the bronze medal boat from New Zealand had been through some of her own struggles and she shouted out so loudly that everyone heard her words: "Silken, just enjoy being so good. You can do it." I knew that all these athletes were recognizing my inner struggle. That support meant so much to me.

During the warm-up, I got determined. I was going to perform at the top of my ability, win or lose. I was going to go out fighting. In the starting gates I was like a cat about to spring. When the gun went off, I took off and rowed with reckless abandon. My race plan went out the window – there was no time for analysis and studied performance. I had to push myself through my own fears and my own doubts. The race went by in a flash and I crossed the finish line second in the world. I have never been so happy, so relieved with a performance. When I got into the dock after the race, my husband, John, ran up to me screaming a victory yell – both of us knew we had exorcised the demon. I wasn't the winner of this race but I had experienced my own personal victory. I never won another World Championship gold medal but my greatest memories of sport are of the personal battles and challenges I faced and conquered. There is more than one way to win a race.

SILKEN LAUMANN was a rower on Canada's Olympic Team at the Olympic Games in Los Angeles, 1984, where she won her first Olympic medal in Double Sculls. She is best known for her Olympic performance in Barcelona, 1992, where she fought back from a near career-ending accident to win a bronze medal. She also won a silver medal at the Olympic Games in Atlanta, 1996.

JOHN PRZYBYSZEWSKI

I have been playing volleyball with a prosthetic leg for 13 years. From indoor to beach, I've participated in many men's and co-ed tournaments over the years. One tournament that sticks out in my mind took place in Toronto a few years ago. My wife and I were playing in a co-ed tournament, and I was wearing a prosthetic leg I had just received the day before. Like a pair of shoes, a prosthetic leg has a "break-in" period. This leg felt much different from the one I had been wearing for the last couple of years. Before our first match, our team began to warm up with a spiking drill. I went up to the net to hit the ball and landed on my good foot, realizing that my artificial leg had broken off and was now lying across the court. The whole gym went silent. You could hear a pin drop. Acting nonchalantly, I picked up my leg, put it back on, and went back to the hitting line. No one at this tournament had noticed I had one leg until then. Now I know what to do if I ever need to get someone's attention.

JOHN PRZYBYSZEWSKI was a silver medallist at the Paralympic Games in Sydney, 2000. He has been a member of Team Canada Disabled Volleyball since 1989.

· 3 ·

THE PAIN OF IT ALL

My teammate and I went through excruciating training to develop the power to move our boat better. The training is simply called "hops." Sounds innocent, easy, something just about anyone could do, right? Try it only if you are really tough and have solid knees.

Fill a sack or old inner tube with 20 pounds of sand and then throw it over your shoulders. Find a nice grassy, spongy place for the workout. Holding each end of the sack, do full squat jumps for 20 seconds then rest for 10 seconds. Repeat this continuously for five minutes. Take a five-minute rest. Do four more sets of five minutes. You will know you have followed the program correctly if you are unable to make your way down a set of stairs in the next hour.

– Susan Antoft, member of Canada's Rowing Team, Olympic Games, Montreal, 1976, and Moscow, 1980 (boycotted Games), and silver medallist, World Championships, New Zealand, 1978

KRISTINA GROVES

During my first season on the international speed skating circuit, I qualified to skate at the World All-Round Championships in February 1999. I made my way to Hamar, Norway, with the rest of the team. My mother, who is from Norway, came along to watch me race and visit with her family. This was my first World Championships and I was excited. Worlds are the biggest competition of the year and it was great to be a part of it, especially having my mother and family there to watch.

I was ready for this competition. I was skating fast, felt good, and was peaking at just the right time. The first day of racing included the 500 metres and the 3,000 metres. I raced well, achieving a personal best in each race, and by a full four seconds in the 3,000 metres. I was extremely happy with my results. The second day of racing included the 1,500 metres and the 5,000 metres, if you qualified.

Let me tell you something about the 1,500 metres. In my opinion, it's the hardest race there is in speed skating. It's neither a full-out sprint nor a paced long distance. It is pure middle-distance pain. By the time you're through, there is so much lactic acid in your system you think you'd rather die than live through it. It's that much fun. Sometimes the lactic acid pools in your stomach and the body's only reaction is to get rid of it as fast as it can: by throwing up. I had often seen skaters throwing up over the mats or into a garbage can after a 1,500-metre race. It's a strange thing, though, I can get through a really great 1,500 metres and feel totally fine after, or I can be out of commission for a few hours afterwards. I just never know how it's going to be.

I was coming off a great day of racing the day before and still felt strong. I had nothing to lose, and my attitude going into the 1,500 metres was to just go for it. When the gun went off, I went into autopilot. My lap times showed I was having a great race and I fought through the pain all the way to the finish. Crossing the line, I was ecstatic to see that I had achieved yet another personal best time. I smiled and waved to my mum and gave my coach a high-five down the back straight. And then it hit me. It's a complete body shutdown and all you want to do is stop and lie down and never get up again, but you know that if you do you *will* never get up again. With every step I could feel my legs expanding, and with every move my stomach was filling. I knew it was coming. There was nothing I could do. I tried to skate around a bit to ward it off but it was no use. I managed to sit on a bench on the inside of the track. And there, with my elbows on my knees and my head hanging down, I waited.

There is really nothing nice to be said about throwing up. It's painful, and it just plain smells. How nice, I thought, to be throwing up in front of 5,000 fans at the World Championships – might as well spread the wealth, put on a show! I could feel the splatter of my vomit bouncing off the ice and hitting my ankles, which made me want to throw up even more. When I finally managed to muster the strength to lift my head, I was looking into the huge lens of a TV camera, broadcasting my "performance" to all of Europe and beyond. How mortified I was! I can just imagine what people must have thought. I bet it wasn't "Hey honey, how 'bout we try that speed skating, it sure looks like fun!" or "Hey, come look at the girl barfing on TV!"

I hope what they really saw was the true test of athleticism, the test of how far one will push oneself to achieve the very best. They didn't see the glorified perfection of every athlete, but the true spirit of personal accomplishment and success. Looking down that camera lens, in my delirious stupor, I *wanted* to believe that's what they saw – my ability to conquer pain and achieve greatness – it's a stretch I know, but sometimes lactic acid will do that to a person!

I imagine I will again one day push myself so hard that I throw up from total effort and exertion. But the pain of going through that brief, insignificant moment will not come close to the pain of knowing that if I hadn't, I wouldn't have done everything I could to skate as fast as I can.

KRISTINA GROVES has been a member of the Canadian National Speed Skating Team for four years. She holds the Canadian speed skating record in the 5,000 metres.

AKOS SANDOR

W hat a year 1997 was! It was like a roller-coaster ride at
     Disneyland. It was also a breakthrough year for me in
the sport of Olympic-style weightlifting but it included a
humorous bump along the way.

I was preparing to attend the World Junior Championships in Cape Town, South Africa, with my coach, who is also
my father. We wanted this experience to be the best it could
be. I'd had some injuries, but they were now behind me and
after a lot of heavy training, while working full-time, going
to school once a week, and studying, I was going to get some
rest in Cape Town before the competition started. My event
would not start until a week after we'd arrived.

In Cape Town, after the team's first training sessions, I felt
good so I decided to use my video camera to film some of the
beautiful landscapes around us. I got about 10 minutes of
footage before the video camera broke but I had another,
potentially more serious, problem. My ring finger had swollen
so badly that I couldn't bend it. Some kind of infection was
under the skin and it looked as if my competition could be a
write-off. Not willing to give up yet, I went to the International Federation's medical commission. Luckily they had
some antibiotics on hand and also recommended that I use
glass to rub on the infected area to speed up the healing. I
went up to my hotel room looking for something made of
glass. The best thing seemed to be an ashtray so I started
rubbing it on my finger. I took the ashtray everywhere I went.
My teammates were looking at me oddly, and other people
were too because I was rubbing the ashtray on my ring finger
all the time to get the swelling down. I took this ashtray

everywhere with me – to training, to the cafeteria, to the competition place, always rubbing the finger.

After two days I didn't feel any improvement was being made, so I went back to the medical commission to tell them that this glass treatment was not working. I showed them the type of glass I was using and asked if it was the right kind. They were in shock when they saw what I was using. They had meant to say "Use ice" but they were mixing up the languages and had used the French word – *glace*. Since I don't speak French, I had thought they meant glass! After two days wasted on this misunderstanding, I finally was able to get the swelling down with *ice* and continued the last-minute preparations for my competition.

The rest of the competition was good for me – I took home one silver and two bronze medals, achieving what I had set out to do: to make the contest the best it could be for me. You might say the medals were just the "icing" on the cake!

AKOS SANDOR won a gold medal in Weightlifting at the Commonwealth Games in Kuala Lumpur, 1998, and was a member of Canada's Pan American Games Team in 1999.

MARK SIMMONS

I vividly remember the day my dad and I stepped into the Toronto Newsboys Boxing Club in downtown Toronto. I was five. A boxing gym is a funny place to be in, because it attracts all types of characters, from hardened criminals to lawyers and police officers, but there were always the young up-and-coming boxers aspiring to become Olympians. In reality, few ever made it out of the local circuit and even fewer boxed nationally.

I loved boxing. No other sport matched me with another opponent equal in size, age, and ability. I felt on an equal playing field with other boxers, something I never experienced in other sports.

I was a small, quiet, and shy kid, and kept to myself a lot, always dreaming of one day becoming an Olympian. However, at 18, I went to the Nationals and placed second in the country. After going on a growth spurt, I stood 6 foot 3½ inches and weighed 201 pounds. I became a heavyweight and again was second best in the country for the next three years.

In 1996 I narrowly lost my bid to get on the Canadian Olympic Team. I almost quit that year, but couldn't look myself in the mirror thinking that I had spent 17 years in this sport and wouldn't realize my dream. Sometimes losing is one of life's greatest lessons as it makes us stronger and even more motivated. I believed it was my destiny and finally I became the Canadian Heavyweight Champion.

For the next four years, I retained my national title and travelled with the team to over 20 countries, winning several gold, silver, and bronze medals. But when I became national champion in 2000, there was no guarantee I would go to the Olympics. In boxing, you have to qualify internationally in order to get to the Olympics. Canada was in a region where there were a possible 40 countries vying for only two spots in the heavyweight division at the Olympics. If I qualified, I would be one of 16 boxers from around the world to compete at the Olympics in my weight division.

Finally it came down to one tournament in Tijuana,

Mexico. The winner would get the final spot to the Olympics. I knew this would be my last opportunity to make it to the Olympics.

In boxing tournaments losing is automatic elimination. In the quarterfinals I had easily defeated a boxer from Venezuela but during the match, I had injured my right hand. After the match, it was clear I had broken it – it had swollen to double its normal size. Back in the hotel room, I soaked my hand in ice, not knowing whether I could box in my semifinal match. I was devastated, but I had to focus and forget about the pain.

The toughest thing about boxing is not the physical aspect, but the mental one – if you believe that you can, you will – and that is what I concentrated on. In my semifinal match, against a cagey boxer from Puerto Rico, I used only my left hand, peppering him with ferocious left jabs and hooks. He could not do anything as I danced my way to a 4–1 victory on points. It was now down to the finals, where I would meet a very tough and strong fighter from Brazil, who had just knocked out his previous two opponents. I knew that to beat him, I would have to use both hands.

The pain in my hand was immense. I could barely close it, let alone punch with it. My body said I couldn't do it, but my mind said I would. Twenty-one years of boxing all came down to this one fight. As I looked across the ring, I saw a bull. His arms were twice mine, his legs were the size of tree trunks, and the look in his eyes was of a warrior. In my corner I bounced confidently, knowing I had the fastest hands in the world, even if one was broken, and knowing I was much more skilful than my opponent. The Brazilian didn't know I had broken my hand, nor did he know how scared I was. It wasn't so much that I was scared of him, but scared of losing, scared that I would disappoint everyone who had supported me over the years, mostly my father, who eagerly waited by the phone at home.

It was a war from the beginning to end. The pain radiated up my arm when I threw my right hand, but I was landing solid blows. At the end it was I who held my hands aloft in victory. I was going to the Olympics.

What a feeling to walk down through that tunnel and enter the stadium for Opening Ceremonies knowing you had the whole country back home supporting you. It was even a greater feeling to win my first Olympic boxing match over Iran. My Olympic dream didn't end with a medal around my neck, but I did place seventh in the world. I can now walk away and cherish my Olympic experience for the rest of my life knowing that all the sacrifices I made were well worth it.

MARK SIMMONS was a member of Canada's Olympic Team, in the Heavyweight Boxing category at the Olympic Games, Sydney, 2000. He was the gold medallist at the Commonwealth Games, 1998.

FABIENNE RAPHAËL

Sunday, August 9, 1999. I remember it as if it were yesterday. The last seconds of the game, ticking down, five – four – three – two – one . . . the buzzer. Final score: Brazil 31, Canada 27. It was over. Our Olympic chance had just . . . gone. The Brazilian girls were running all over with their Brazilian flag. Brazilian fans were screaming and congratulating their athletes. My team, on the opposite side of that Pan American Games Convention Centre handball court, was defeated.

We could have made a river with our tears. The Canadian fans were stunned. This game was the most important of our lives. It was the only opportunity for us to qualify for the 2000 Olympic Games in Sydney, Australia. Gold. That's what we had to win. Not silver. Gold would have been the synonym for happiness, accomplishment, money, visibility. Silver was the synonym for tears, failure, broken heart – worse than anything that ever happened to me in my entire life.

The previous three years had been filled with hard training, training camps, injuries, searching for sponsors, sacrifice, discipline, amassing the $1,250 we would have to pay in order to represent our country. I was a full-time physiotherapy student, but I had to find time to do my three-times-a-week cardio, three-times-a-week weightlifting, and five-times-a-week handball. It was a lot, but I was focused, so it became easier. I visualized my team winning the Pan Am finals. Sunday, August 9, 1999, was a reminder that life can sometimes be cruel.

For a long time after the Pan Ams, I thought that nothing else mattered in my life. I felt that I was about to fail at everything I wanted to accomplish, as if a witch had cast a bad spell over me – low self-esteem, tears, pain, desolation – but my brother Patrick, my friend and teammate Nathalie, and of course my love of handball helped me through those rough moments.

Today, although I still feel that something is missing, I don't intend to quit. I have started a project but didn't finish it.

Me and handball? It's a love story that started 11 years ago. We have a thing going on. And you know what? Our love keeps growing every day. Watch out for the two of us. Santo Domingo 2003.

FABIENNE RAPHAËL has been a member of the Senior National Women's Handball Team since 1996.

DANIELLE GOYETTE

I have played hockey for Team Canada since 1992 and for me, it was a big part of my life – it *was* my life – until 1998.

I had the opportunity to play with the Women's Olympic Team in Nagano. At the end of January we travelled to Japan to prepare for the Olympic Winter Games by playing some exhibition games, practising, and getting used to the time change. I had been looking forward to this trip for a long time. I had fought some injuries throughout the winter and was now feeling rested and healthy. I wanted nothing more than to play hockey in the Olympic Games!

Three days before the Opening Ceremonies I started to feel different. I wasn't playing well, I was very moody, and I just wanted to be alone. I didn't know what was happening to me but I knew something was wrong. Then the day before the ceremonies, my best friend on the team told me our coach wanted to talk to me. I said I didn't want to talk, I wanted to be left alone. I thought the coach wanted to talk about my lack of desire to play. I couldn't have been more wrong! I went to the coach's room, and as soon as I went in, I knew.

My father had been sick with Alzheimer's disease over the past few years and three days ago, he had taken a turn for the worse. He had just passed away. Immediately memories of my mum came back to me – in 1996, three days before the National Championship, she had passed away.

For the next 24 hours, I was on the phone with my family and crying a lot. The most important person in my life was now gone – I didn't know what to do. My family wanted me to stay in Nagano, because they knew how hard I had worked to be there. They said our dad was in a better place now and he would still see me play. I decided to stay and play hockey but my heart was with my family.

The next two weeks were a blur. I went to the rink, played our game, and returned to my room to be alone and cry. I didn't want my teammates to see me upset, so I tried my best to be normal and asked them to treat me the same but inside, my heart was broken. The media hounded us for interviews but I refused them for the first three days. I did not want to discuss my dad, because I needed to concentrate on playing hockey, and so did my teammates.

Throughout the Games, however, I never stopped thinking about my dad. There was a piece of nylon that had come loose on my skate and whenever I returned to the bench I would look down at that piece of nylon. This would be my signal to focus on the game – I was now playing for my dad. We went on to win the silver medal, and although my Olympic experience was not what I thought it would be, it changed my life forever.

Hockey is still a big part of my life, but I look at life differently and I look at sport differently – I challenge myself to be the best I can be, both in hockey and in other areas of my life. My ambition is to play in another Olympic Games, knowing my parents are still watching me.

DANIELLE GOYETTE was on the silver medal team for Canada in Ice Hockey at the Olympic Winter Games in Nagano, 1998. She has six gold medals with Team Canada at the World Championships and is the all-time leading goal scorer with Team Canada in international competition.

·4·

OPPORTUNITY KNOCKS

*I got into fencing because of the movie The Princess Bride –
the movie made it look like fun! So when a woman was trying
to recruit athletes for wheelchair fencing one day, I joined.
From The Princess Bride to the gold medal at the North
American Championships in Wheelchair Fencing – wow!*

– Sylvie Morel, member of Canada's Paralympic Team,
Wheelchair Fencing, Sydney, 2000

DAVE O'DONNELL

It was a hot summer day, and the fencing team was out at one of its usual practices. This particular year, an exchange student who had studied fencing for a number of years in Europe was fencing here in Canada with a Canadian coach. The Canadians weren't known for being great fencers in the European community, an attitude that was reflected in the behaviour of the exchange student. He was having difficulty with the new coaching style and doubted some of the moves and philosophies of the coach.

During the summer, the gym doors are often open to allow the breeze into the room. The coach and the exchange student were working away practising various blade techniques. Partway through the lesson the coach was reviewing the material they had just practised. As with most summer days when the doors are open, a number of flies were buzzing around, generally making a nuisance of themselves. One adventurous fly settled on the floor near where student and coach were talking. The lesson that day had been a difficult one dealing with accuracy and control. And once again the coach could sense some resistance.

As they paused, their attention was drawn to a fly that continued to buzz around their sabre tips that were pointing to and touching the floor. For some reason, their attention was fixated on the fly, the floor, and the tips of the sabres. In a flash, the coach's weapon lashed out toward the fly, standing on the floor only a few inches away. There was a pause, except for the lightning movement of the sword. The fly remained standing in exactly the same position it had been before the move. Then, almost as if in slow motion, the fly's head fell to the ground and the body keeled over backwards. The coach looked up at the student, who was slowly rubbing his chin between his thumb and forefinger, mesmerized by what he had just witnessed. He turned his head in the direction of the coach, their eyes met, there was silence, and then the student uttered almost under his breath, "I think I have a lot more respect for you now!" They smiled and continued with their work.

DAVE O'DONNELL is the head fencing coach at McMaster University. He has also coached and managed at the Canada Winter Games in 1991, 1995, and 1999 and was assistant coach and manager for the National Team in 1987 and 1988. He fenced competitively at regional, provincial, and national levels.

JOHN CHILD AND MARK HEESE

It was a typical mid-January morning as we awoke at 6:00 a.m. to go to work. I called over to John to get up because we had an important job to do that day. I quickly walked over to the window to check the temperature on the giant digital thermometer across the street. As I read the thermometer I thought to myself that it wasn't too bad today, and I turned to John and said, "Mother Nature must be on our side today, it's only 35°C." So we grabbed our shades, shorts, and sunscreen and headed to the beach!

Let me clarify a few things: First, the beach was Copacabana Beach in Rio de Janeiro. Second, John and I were there for the World Beach Volleyball Championships in 1996. The temperature was "only" 35°C because it was five degrees cooler than the previous morning. And last, I admit to stretching the truth when I called "heading to the beach for a tournament" work.

However, at that time of year we usually do have our work cut out for us, simply because of the extreme conditions. The elements don't usually work to our advantage when we play in Brazil in January. We are coming from much cooler temperatures in Canada, where we're forced to practise indoors without sun, wind, or any other hazardous conditions. The Brazilians, on the other hand, are quite used to the heat and enjoy home-court advantage with thousands of fans coming to cheer them on. We are accustomed to having to play in front of a hostile Brazilian crowd, but on this day, strangely enough, it was the Brazilians who would have to fight off the elements and deal with some unfriendly visitors.

We began the day with a win against the Spaniards, which put us one win away from the semifinals. We then faced the top-ranked team, Franco-Roberto of Brazil, in our fourth-round game. With the crowd behind them and the rising temperature getting to us, we were outplayed by a score of 15–11.

However, beach volleyball tournaments are played with a double elimination format, which means we have to lose two matches before we're finished. We had one more chance. As we waited to see who we would play, we tried to cool off in the enclosed air-conditioned players' tent. The temperature had risen to 44°C. Finally, we learned that we would be facing another Brazilian team, Moreira-Garrido.

During the warm-up, the Brazilian players were crushing hits and serves, which indicated that they weren't at all affected by the heat. Despite feeling we were in over our heads, we dragged our tired and sunburned bodies onto the court. The thousands of Brazilian fans booed and heckled us almost immediately. The game began with a service ace by Garrido, which was followed by two digs and point conversions by Moreira. It was 3−0 before we even had a chance to serve! The Brazilians continued pretty much to dominate the game, and despite our making a few decent plays here and there, they were soon up 14−9 with match point. We called a time-out. We stalled for as long as possible, and then called for another time-out. We were trying to break their momentum, and then perhaps come back on the court and make one last push for a comeback. Comebacks in beach volleyball are fairly common, and we knew that anything could happen. And anything did happen.

As we headed back to the court, we noticed that one of the Brazilian players was running hysterically around his time-out area. As well, the referee was descending from his referee's stand in an unusually frantic manner. John and I retreated to the far end of the stadium as we watched this strange scenario unfold. A large swarm of bees had entered the stadium area and were buzzing around the Brazilian players and attaching themselves to the referee's stand a few metres away. After several minutes, the bees had completely covered the referee's stand and had finally stopped harassing the Brazilian players, who had found their way into the player's tent. As the tournament officials were scrambling to find a solution to this bizarre situation, an Italian player, who claimed to have studied animal biology, explained to John and me that bees are attracted to the colour blue. Who was I to argue, because sure enough, the referee's stand was painted a deep blue, and the Brazilians were wearing dark blue hats! The good ol' Canadian colours of red and white on our uniforms certainly came in handy that day.

After a half-hour of unsuccessful attempts to shoo the bees away, the fire department was called to come and spray the stand with a special chemical. It worked and the bees buzzed off as quickly as they came. Play resumed a short while later. However, the crowd had filed out because they assumed the game was over, and likely didn't want to get stung. It didn't seem like a big deal at the time, but when we noticed that the Brazilian players looked quite frazzled about the ordeal, we knew we had a chance. Sure enough, they immediately served match point into the net to give service back to us. We went on to score seven unanswered points to win the game 16–14 and make it into the semifinals!

Mother Nature was on our side after all, as her swarm of bees played a huge role in what turned out to be a World Championship bronze medal. It may sound silly and superstitious, but during our numerous tournaments in Brazil since 1996, we've always showed our thanks to the Brazilian bees by spreading honey on our morning toast.

JOHN CHILD and MARK HEESE were bronze medallists in Beach Volleyball at the Olympic Games in Atlanta, 1996. They were also members of Canada's Beach Volleyball Team at the Olympic Games in Sydney, 2000.

JENNIFER ROBINSON

Just five days before we were to leave for Nice, France, in 2000, for the World Figure Skating Championships, I was cleaning my townhouse and as I ran up the stairs two at a time I jumped on a piece of broken glass – barefoot. Just underneath the toes on my left foot was a bleeding gash. I was frantic! I asked the doctor not to use stitches to treat it because I was worried it would irritate my foot in my skate. He cleaned up the cut and sent me home. I had one day of rest before training would start again.

On Monday morning I stepped on the ice, my foot swollen from the cut. This turned out to be a blessing in disguise. The main reason I had finished so low in international competitions was my unfortunate habit of landing my jumps on two feet when you are supposed to land only on your right foot. Because of my cut, it was more painful to land on two feet and now I was consistently completing clean run-throughs and jumps!

In Nice, I gave the best performance of my career, finishing eighth in the world, and 10 spots higher than my last finish at a World Championships. This standing secured a spot for a second woman for the next year's World Championships in Vancouver. Two Canadian women had not competed together at a World Championship in five years! It gave me a whole new perspective on injuries!

JENNIFER ROBINSON is a figure skater and has been the Canadian National Champion for four years.

PHILIPPE LaROCHE

By 1994 I had won an Olympic gold medal in Albertville, in aerial freestyle skiing, and an Olympic silver in Lillehammer. It was a perfect time to retire. I was on a high and felt I could go no higher. The following year I began coaching and was content to stay retired, but some friends who I was coaching convinced me to compete again in 1995 at the World Championships in France because as World Champion from the previous year I would not have to qualify to do so. I would be competing against them as well, but they said it would be fun, a time to compete together – it was also my last call for the romance of it all.

In the aerial competition of freestyle, you have to do two jumps in the semifinals, and if you qualify in the top 12 you go through to the final the next day. Before the competition, I was feeling great because I knew it was my last one and I intended to savour every minute. Although I was a little nervous, my goal was not to win but to have fun and enjoy the ride.

First I had to qualify in the semifinal. All the skiers were divided into two groups – the A group and the B group. The A group comprised the top 20 on the World Cup circuit determined by the current-year results. Group A was always given the best time of day to compete and the best conditions – less wind, sunny skies, no shadows, no darkness. . . . But I was in the B group for the first time in years because I had not participated in any World Cup competitions that year. The A group finished in the early part of the day but the B group didn't start until 4 p.m. The sun had left the valley where the competition was being held about an hour before that! Although there was still daylight, by 4:00 it was fading – fast.

My first jump at 4:30 was good but I was not sure it was good enough. At 5:30, as the final jumper of the day, I prepared to do my second and last jump. It was now almost completely dark, and I could not see very well – a definite hazard in aerial jumping. This was the challenge of my career – a difficult jump in difficult conditions, with all the younger skiers watching, many of them rookies on the circuit. I was 29, and most of them were between 17 and 23.

I took a deep breath and jumped. It was exhilarating! Everything came together for me. I did well enough to qualify for the finals the next day. In fact I was in third place. It was like winning the Olympics! I had competed beside younger kids who were competing for the very first time for the World Cup. They were so proud of me and that was as rewarding as winning my Olympic medals.

The next day, everything went wrong.

I lost my helmet in the air in the first jump. I landed on my back, not on my skis, which is the worst thing you can do. I bent my knee on the jump, so instead of going high I went further down the hill, which is disastrous.

Any other year, at any other race, I would have been angry at myself for failing so badly, but this time was different.

This time I was totally relaxed, happy, and laughing. Laughing at myself. The day before I had already achieved my goal and that was my challenge. It was for me a great ending to a wonderful career.

I finished eighth that day but in my heart I felt first . . . I had finished my career in good shape, physically and mentally. The media was all around as I reminisced about my career and final race and I remember so vividly that it was sunny. I was happy to end on a sunny day and will never forget my challenge in the dark.

PHILIPPE LaROCHE won a gold medal in Freestyle Skiing at the Olympic Winter Games in Albertville, 1992, and a silver medal in Lillehammer, 1994.

ROB RUSNOV

It was January of my first year in high school when I heard an announcement over the PA one morning about the archery team. I immediately went to the library and pulled out the *Guinness Book of World Records* to see if it was an Olympic sport. Ever since Grade 5, when I'd been forced to do a project on the Olympic Games in Sarajevo, I had an Olympic dream. At the time it didn't matter what the sport was, I just wanted the glory of competing for my country in the Olympic Games. As it turned out, archery is an Olympic sport. I went home that night and announced to my parents that I was going to the Olympics for archery, without ever having shot a bow. Well, that's not exactly true. My best friend and I used to go into our neighbourhood ravine, chop down trees, and make bows and arrows. With our bows we would try to shoot unsuspecting birds – thankfully we never hit any.

ROB RUSNOV was a member of Canada's Archery Team at the Olympic Games in Atlanta, 1996, and Sydney, 2000.

· 5 ·

BEYOND THE BARRIERS

A group of us were on our way to compete in the Eastern Canadian Track and Field Championships in St.-Lambert, Quebec. In Montreal, a taxi crashed into our car, pinning us against a building. We were taken by ambulance to the Royal Victoria Hospital, with "superficial bruises and shock." For the rest of the night, I was awakened every three hours as there was some concern that I had suffered a slight concussion. But I was determined to qualify for the British Empire Games, so I showed up for the 440-yard race the next day as scheduled — and won!

– Cecelia Carter-Smith, member of the Canadian Track and Field Team at the British Empire and Commonwealth Games, 1966, and the British Commonwealth Games, 1970

JEFF ADAMS

I'll never forget the time or the place: noon, August 20, 1992, at the Olympic Games in Barcelona, Spain. I was getting ready to race in the final of the 1,500-metre wheelchair race, a demonstration event at the Olympics. Every few moments, everything around me seemed to rumble, and a tremendous roar filled the air. The other competitors and I were all wearing our race faces, trying to act tough and confident.

We were all scared to death.

At least I was.

I had been training for this day for six years, and the road to qualify for this particular event had not been easy. At the Olympic Trials in Louisiana I almost didn't qualify. I had been anxious and nervous. There were some guys in strong shape that year. I remember watching Jean-Marc Bercet from Switzerland turn endless warm-up laps at close to race pace. The defending champion, a legend of wheelchair racing, Mustapha Badid from France, intimidated whoever came near him. The athlete I looked up to most was my teammate, André Viger. He was quietly and efficiently warming up as he prepared for his heat, not saying much to anyone. He wheeled past where I was stretching and threw me a wink.

I watched the competitors line up and felt I had hardly blinked or taken a breath before I saw André finish fifth – he would not progress to the quarterfinals. My breathing started again – I might have been hyperventilating – as Mustapha also went down in the prelims. Now I was really nervous. Nevertheless, a sudden and complete calm descended on me when my coach, Peter Eriksson, put his hand on my shoulder and said, "You got these guys, champ – just race your race."

We both knew what that meant. Peter had drilled it into my head, through strategy sessions, and killer quarter-mile repeats for the last 18 months.

The gun went off, and everything fell into place. I got in behind Jean-Marc Bercet, who set a furious pace for the first two laps. With 400 metres to go, just as the bell rang, I started to hammer. Going into the last 100 metres, I was in the lead and feeling great. I straightened out and headed for the finish line. I glanced over my left shoulder, to make sure no one was trying to move on my inside, glanced over my right shoulder, and no one was there either.

With about 10 metres to go before the finish line, the nerves, the fear – I don't know what else – all came together. I put my arms up, to celebrate, more out of relief than anything.

With my arms up in the air, I was passed. At first, I thought *three* racers had passed me, but in a photo of the finish, it was decided I had finished third – by 3/100 of a second.

André came up to me after the results had been displayed. I thought he was coming to wish me luck in the quarterfinals the next day or to talk about his race. He was actually coming to take my head off.

He screamed at me in English and French for what seemed like an eternity. He told me that he expected his training partners and teammates to treat themselves with respect, and that what I had done was the most disrespectful thing he had ever seen. Disrespectful to myself, and to the other athletes I was racing against.

It was the wake-up call I needed. Now here I was, three weeks later, in Barcelona, preparing to race in the final at the Olympics. I was in the best shape of my career.

We were taken out of the warm-up area, and the stadium walls shook again, and a roar like the sound of a fighter jet almost deafened us, echoing off the concrete of the underbelly of the stadium. I realized that the roar was the crowd screaming, and the rumbling was the feet of 60,000 fans stamping on the stands.

It was then that I fully realized what the Olympics and the Paralympics are really about. They're about something so incredible happening, a moment of such excellence, that an entire stadium full of people have no choice but to open their mouths and scream.

But I still had to prove myself, and my lessons were far from over. With 300 metres to go in my race, the right push ring came off my wheel. It was something I've never seen happen to anyone else. It meant I had no way of pushing my racing chair to the finish line. When I felt my wheel break and saw the push ring roll off the track, I decided to stop. I'd had enough. After six years of hard work, after the lessons in Louisiana, after realizing what the Olympics really were about, it was just too much. It wasn't fair. I started to pull over.

In that same moment, something changed. I thought again – after six years of hard work, after the lessons in Louisiana, after realizing what the Olympics really were about – damned if I was going to stop before I finished what I had started.

So I finished. I finished last, but I finished.

A week later, I refocused, remotivated myself, and went on to win a silver medal in the 800 metres at the Paralympics, on the same track that I "lost" at during the demonstration event at the Olympics. Since then, I've competed in every major event in the world and won my share of medals, including two gold medals in the Paralympic Games in Sydney.

I couldn't have done any of that if I had quit that day in Barcelona. All I had learned through sport came together in that moment on the track. My moment of excellence had nothing to do with crossing the finish line first. It had to do with taking a bad thing and using it to motivate myself; it had to do with turning bad into good.

Turning bad to good is like turning coal into diamonds, and it's something we can all try to do every day. I can't think of a more valiant struggle, or a more beautiful victory.

JEFF ADAMS won two gold medals, one silver, and two bronze in Wheelchair Racing at the Paralympic Games in Sydney, 2000. He was also gold, silver, and bronze medallist at the Paralympic Games in Atlanta, 1996. He has represented Canada twice at the Olympics in demonstration events.

SANDRA LEVY

As a black Canadian athlete, I was not remotely interested in visiting South Africa, with its white-ruled and racist apartheid government. Despite that, in 1993, I spent six weeks training in Durban, South Africa. I describe the tour as one in which I went in with a chip on my shoulder and came out with the lumberyard. Despite the tour's shortcomings, it was a growth experience.

In 1992, international sanctions against South Africa had been lifted, allowing South Africa once again to compete in the Olympic Games. (South Africa had not competed as a nation in the Olympics since 1960.) On April 27, 1993, exactly one year before South Africa's first ever multiracial election, my team – the Canadian women's field hockey team – travelled to South Africa to train against the South African women's field hockey team.

We had chosen South Africa as a training site first to acclimatize for the upcoming World Cup qualifying tournament and second to experience the expected strong competition from the South African players. South Africa proved to be a great training site. The tough, fast, and skilled South African competition helped our development as a team.

I had had strong reservations about going to South Africa largely because I had supported sanctions against South Africa since my teenage years. I was anxious about how I would be treated by South Africans, both black and white. I was concerned about the violence that had been reported by the media following the murder of African National Congress member Chris Hani. How would I be treated in restaurants – would I even be allowed to enter?

The trip started off poorly. On my connecting flight from London to Johannesburg, I was seated beside a middle-aged, white South African woman who made it clear she was not pleased to be in the same row as me. In Afrikaans, she asked the stewardess to move me to another seat. Apparently, the stewardess told her that she was welcome to move to an empty seat, which further perturbed her. This woman remained in her seat and we endured each other for 11 hours.

In Durban, a white male bus driver drove us to our hotel. The driver got several black male porters to assist us with our luggage. After removing our luggage from the bus, the porters waved a thumbs-up sign to the driver, smiled, and yelled, "Yea baas!" The *yea baas* immediately conjured up images of slave and master in my mind. My excitement was dwindling quickly.

The first week in South Africa was particularly challenging. My teammates and I were part of a crowd of 60,000 spectators attending a rugby match at a local stadium on day two of our tour. Natal Province was playing an Australian state side. I was shocked by a few stinging racial slurs that were directed at me and even more by the commonplace derogatory comments uttered within earshot. I had never been subjected to such overt racism.

In general, though, South Africans of all shades treated me with polite indifference. The few black people I interacted with were cool and distant because they only ever saw me with white people. White people engaged me in obligatory safe non-political conversation, and revealed to me with obvious surprise that I was not like their blacks. The Indian population in Durban, which is predominantly Muslim, is the largest East Indian population outside of India. These Indians were friendly. They recognized me as American and felt solidarity with American blacks because of the strong Black Muslim conversion during the black civil rights movement in the 1960s.

I did not allow my fears of rejection to stop me completely from socializing at night. I went out for dinners and to bars and clubs with my teammates from time to time. Although I was never turned away from any public establishment, I did not always feel welcome.

I was lonely and angry for much of the six weeks. Some of my loneliness was self-imposed. I isolated myself from my teammates and chose not to attend some functions. My anger was rooted in my frustration over the apartheid situation in South Africa and its impact on me and my inability to have an impact on it. Interestingly, I played exceptionally well on this tour. In practice games I was often recognized for my outstanding play. Perhaps I felt I had something to prove.

On reflection, I believe that I did have an impact. I believe that I showed the few South Africans who I met what a black person can achieve when afforded opportunities that are supposed to be available to all people in a free and democratic country.

SANDRA LEVY was a member of Canada's Field Hockey Team at the Olympic Games in Seoul, 1988, and Barcelona, 1992.

JOE NG

In the prime of my table tennis career at the age of 23, I was diagnosed with later-stage cancer.

The doctors had told me I had a 30-per-cent chance of surviving cancer-free and a 70-per-cent chance of the cancer spreading, leaving me with only a few years to live. I was in a daze for a couple of weeks. It was in the middle of winter, and very cold, yet every night I went to the Beaches in Toronto and just walked along the boardwalk, my mind trying to grapple with this blow. After a couple of weeks of this, I said to myself, everybody's got to go sometime but I'm going to fight this the best I can. Once I accepted the possibility of death I was better prepared to do battle.

I underwent surgery in November to remove my thymus gland and my upper left lung, then had three sessions of chemotherapy. I also used some non-traditional therapies of vitamins and herbs, as well as mental imagery. I tried everything.

After my last session of chemotherapy I just wanted to get back into life and back to the game I loved. I refused to let the illness consume me. I remember bouncing the ball on my racquet and against the wall in my hospital room while lying in bed after surgery. I was probably driving the nurses crazy! When I was out of the hospital, I set higher goals for myself and didn't feel any limitations. My main focus was on my health and table tennis, and I knew that I could improve each one through the other.

In April I was invited by my team to go to the World Table Tennis Championships – not as a competitor, but as a spectator, to help the team and cheer them on. But during the tournament, I asked if I could play and I was able to help my team win a couple of matches! That was a turning point for me. All my focus could now be on the game – and on getting stronger.

I've been free of cancer now for 15 years and have competed in three Olympic Games in that time. I never take my health for granted and am always looking for ways to improve it through exercises of the mind and body and a healthy diet.

Sport revived my spirits – and focused my energies. To this day I credit the game for my recovery.

JOE NG was a member of the Canadian Olympic Team in Table Tennis at the Olympic Games in Seoul, 1988, Barcelona, 1992, and Atlanta, 1996.

CHRISSY REDDEN

September 23, 2000 – the date I'd been dreaming about for two years. In the previous six months, I don't believe a day had passed without thoughts of the Olympics.

I was part of the Canadian mountain bike team, sojourning in a small town south of Sydney, Australia, for three weeks before the race. It was an ideal training camp at an ideal time. Two days before the race I was mentally, physically, and tactically as ready as I could be. I knew I had the legs and the head to perform my best in the hardest and toughest race of my career.

On the morning of the race I woke up excited. I had had a good sleep, my legs felt energized, and my teammates were also in a good mood. Not much conversation went on. Each of us knew what the others needed and we all silently wished the best for each other. We went to the course a few hours early to ensure that we would get there no matter what traffic or other difficulties we encountered.

I was able to put in a half lap on the demanding course before the officials closed it to allow the 30,000 spectators access to the best viewing locations. My time was great! I was really excited, but not anxious. I was in a perfect state of stimulation mixed with calm.

With 15 minutes left before the race, the competitors gathered in the staging area. The atmosphere was alive with excitement. Everyone was in her own state of optimal "race face." Each acknowledging smile was met with tenseness. We all wished each other well, but every one of us wanted it for herself.

I got a good spot on the front line and was psyched to attack. The start was blazingly fast! I had expected a fast start but was unprepared for the number of girls going all out until the first bit of single track. At a World Cup, five or six would be contending for that coveted spot. Today, there were about 20 of us. That underestimation cost me a few places, and I went into the single track around sixth place. That first mistake caused me to get stuck behind traffic and I was forced off the bike to jump over a log. It took the rest of the first lap (of five) to get back into my zone. Into the second lap, I started moving forward.

Suddenly I felt something odd – my bike was slowing down. I was attacking up a climb, but the front end was not responding the way it should have. When I looked down to my front wheel, it confirmed one of my worst fears – I had a slow leak.

Within a minute, I would have a completely flat front tire. Immediately, I pulled over and went into "stay calm and fix flat" mode. The fix was fast. As I was working, I was aware of my friends whipping past. I could feel their eyes on me. They might be sorry for my misfortune, but they were glad it hadn't happened to them.

When I jumped back on the bike and started stomping, I was in 15th place. By the time I finished my second lap, I was in 13th place. I knew that a medal was impossible, but I wanted to salvage as much of this race as possible! I knew I had the legs, I still wanted to use them. The next three laps were attack, pass, attack.

When I crossed the finish line I was eighth. After congratulating and commiserating with some other racers, I went back to my bench and started to whip the dust and determination from my face and arms when it dawned on me – I had just finished the Olympics! I had raced as hard as I could. I had flatted. I was eighth. That realization gave me a profound sense of disappointment. The feeling was so powerful it just about knocked me over!

All the passion, training, thought, and energy that had gone into my performance were dissipating. I felt cheated. I also felt that my family, who had flown all the way to Sydney from Binbrook, Ontario, had been cheated. I felt that my coach, Yuri Kashirin, had been cheated. Why was I so unlucky?

As it turned out, I was lucky. The next day my front tire was flat again, this time with two thorns. Indeed, luck *had* been on my side. The tire had lasted long enough for me to finish – and I *had* finished! I reached my goals. I had set out to prepare, to the best of my abilities, and perform 100 per cent on race day. I left the Olympics with two of three goals attained. (The third goal was a medal!)

After my race, my team moved into the village to relax and mingle with the rest of the athletes. I was feeling a little let down with my result and was a little sorry for myself. Preparing for the race had been my entire existence for the past few years, and I had "failed." But in the athletes' village,

I looked around and realized I was among about 7,000 other athletes who were feeling and experiencing the same mixed emotions and reactions as I was. I saw that the race itself was only part of my Olympic story. Putting my experience into perspective helped me understand that the process of getting to and preparing for the race was also part of the event, and the lessons learned getting here were just as important as those learned on race day.

CHRISSY REDDEN was a member of the Canadian Mountain Biking Team at the Olympic Games in Sydney, 2000. She has been a member of the Canadian Mountain Biking Team since 1994.

TANYA TYGESEN

In order for our fencing event to be admitted to a tournament, we had to have at least 10 entries (women compete only against women) in the tournament. Countless times my mother would end up on the entry ballot so that we could have our tournament – she didn't even fence! – and two of the other entries were my sisters, who did fence. The Tygesen girls were a strong contingent in those days! If a tournament got off the ground, we then had to endure the ridicule and curiosity of our male counterparts. Men's épée had been a well-established event until we came along. As the men gathered around the piste (the fencing area made of a 14-metre-long by 1-metre-wide strip of copper) to watch, women épée fencers were laughed at and teased, as the men thought we were using a man's weapon! The first group of women épéeists hung in there and proved that we too could fence épée – I have always thought we were like the suffragettes of the fencing world. *En garde!*

TANYA TYGESEN was the gold medallist at the Commonwealth Games, 1991, member of the Canadian Women's Épée Team from 1983 to 1998, and four-time National Champion.

· 6 ·

THE PRICE OF FAME

*I had been on a bus with Gaetan Boucher. When we got off,
a girl who'd been on the bus also got off. She was looking at
us so I said "Hello!" as she walked over. She timidly asked,
"Isn't that. . .", then stopped and looked at Gaetan, who
had turned around to say hello. "Didn't you use to be
Gaetan Boucher?" she asked. Gaetan smiled politely and
replied, "Yes — and I still am!"*

– Dawn Watson, three-time Canadian Modern Pentathlon
champion

CAROLYN WALDO

I never realized how much Olympic athletes are admired until after I'd competed at the Olympic Games. Following the Seoul Olympics, I gave a lot of speeches to schools all over the country. One talk took me to Edmonton. When I arrived in the elementary school, I realized I had to use the washroom. I asked the principal where the "little girls' room" was – a question that was overheard by about 20 Grade 1 students. They offered to show me where the washroom was. Once we'd arrived at the washroom, I said, "Thank you," hoping they would get the hint to get lost. But oh, no, they wanted to follow Carolyn Waldo into the washroom.

I went into the stall, shut the door, and to my surprise there was silence. Before doing anything at all, I peered down under the door and saw 40 little feet standing there in silence. I quickly realized that they wanted to hear Carolyn Waldo go to the bathroom. I guess their lesson of the day was that I'm not any different than they are! Aren't kids great!

CAROLYN WALDO won two gold medals for Canada in Synchronized Swimming at the Olympic Games in Seoul, 1988.

NICOLAS GILL

I started judo when I was six years old. I'd watched my brother in a local competition in a church basement and that got me into it. My first competition was only two weeks after I started. I lost both matches I was entered in. But I told myself, "Next time, it will be different." I did not know what I was getting myself into but at the age of 20 I finally made it to the Olympics – Barcelona in 1992 – and to the podium.

At the doping control room after the medal presentation, I was already planning to enjoy my Olympic experience. Then a young Spanish man came to me and in terrible French told me that a journalist was waiting for me outside. I had already done two interviews just before so I thought, "Cool – one more interview!" When I was finished in the doping room, I walked out and quickly realized the importance of an Olympic medal: More than 20 journalists and photographers were waiting for me! They were from all over Canada. The next morning I was on the front page of all the major Canadian newspapers: I had won the first medal for Canada in these Olympic Games.

NICOLAS GILL was a silver medallist in Judo at the Olympic Games in Sydney, 2000, and a bronze medallist in Barcelona, 1992. He is also a three-time World medallist.

ALEXANDRE DESPATIE

By the time I was 13, I was the Canadian diving champion and held several senior records. Before that, the youngest senior divers had been 15 or 16 years old. I'd been diving since I was six or seven years old against kids my own age, but my abilities soon took me into the senior ranks. Now, in 1998, I knew I had a chance to go to the Commonwealth Games in Kuala Lumpur. This would be a major step in my diving career. First, though, I had to place at the senior nationals, competing against divers who were older than I, some who had been Canadian champions before, and who, unlike me, had been to international meets before. But I didn't fear my opponents because they were also my friends. In some ways, it was just another day on the diving board, because I was not about to change anything in the way I approached the task – and I was successful.

The day I left Montreal for Kuala Lumpur I certainly didn't know that my life was about to change. I was very excited and very nervous. Not only was this my longest trip by plane – I'd been all across Canada and to Orlando, but I'd never crossed the ocean – but it was also my most important competition ever. I felt like a David with the Goliaths (I say "with" because I was not competing *against* them). My goal in Kuala Lumpur was to do the best I possibly could in these circumstances, get a lot of experience, and most of all enjoy myself and have fun. Already, in spite of my nervousness, I felt I was in the "zone" – the place where we are in total control of ourselves.

When we got to the facilities in Kuala Lumpur, the first thing that impressed me was that we were diving outside. I will never forget the fantastic view from the 10-metre tower that stood right in the middle of the city. But more than that, I quickly realized I was the youngest and smallest guy in the entire Commonwealth Games – I was about 5 feet and 100 pounds (today I'm 5 feet 7 inches and 138 pounds!). The other competitors were 18 years old and up; in diving, the oldest competitor was 28.

Because of the difference in size and age between me and the other competitors, I felt no pressure, knowing that I was there for the experience. My daily training was going really well, and it wasn't hard to remind myself that I wanted to have fun during that week. We had to go through preliminaries and semifinals and I felt very comfortable at those events. In fact, my small size was an advantage – the smaller you are, the faster you can rotate in your figures.

For the final, we were diving at night. You could hear the noise of the streets and see the millions of mini lights from the city. It was a warm evening and although I couldn't see any stars, I remember there was a moon. I was in some sort of bubble, very concentrated on what I had to do. I was still in the zone. I knew where the other divers were during the competition. I like to know what's happening with them because it tells me how much I have to "open the machine," and that night my body was co-operating 100 per cent. To dive from a 10-metre platform is the greatest feeling. You feel like you're flying – it's a feeling of complete freedom. If you decide to open at the right time, it's a great dive. If you decide to open too soon or too late, *smack*. As soon as you touch the water, you know if it's a good dive. So on that night of September 1998, after each dive, I felt it was the best I had ever done. I couldn't believe what was happening . . . it was magical! I had so much fun diving that night!

I had six dives to do and of course did the most difficult ones first. After the third dive, I had accomplished the best scores I'd ever had for these difficult dives so I knew if I went on like that, I had a good chance of getting on the podium. But on my fourth dive – a three-and-a-half-front somersault, my favourite dive – I had a perfect ten! Then I knew I was on my way to the gold if I kept going like that – which I did.

I was absolutely overwhelmed by what I had just accomplished. I had broken the Commonwealth record. As soon as I got out of the water, I saw my coach crying, my good friend Phillipe Comtois was crying, and then I started to cry. Suddenly the pressure was off – I was waving the Canadian flag and crying. Someone gave me a phone so I could talk to my family back home and I was so happy to hear their voices!

That day was a turning point in my life. When I came back home, I was surrounded by journalists, cameras, TV, and people everywhere who suddenly knew "the boy," as they referred to me. I was as amazed as they were and just as excited.

But life goes on. So did school and training . . . but everything was different. Now I was a public figure, and I felt there were expectations I had to live up to.

The 1999 schedule was already planned. The World Cup was coming up in January but although my training was going fairly well, I was finding it a bit hard to concentrate on the future. I was still tired from the thrill of winning at the Commonwealth Games and from the travelling.

Although I was feeling confident and believed I could not dive badly at all, unconsciously my outlook slowly began to change – I would not allow myself many mistakes (like everyone, athletes learn from their mistakes) and tried to make each dive, even in training, perfect. I was aware I had become a role model for the younger divers and I had to live up to that reputation and stay as good as I had been in Kuala Lumpur only a few months before. The pressure was on, and I could feel it but believed I could not show it.

When I arrived in Wellington, New Zealand, for the World Cup, I was in good shape but I could feel that something was different from previous meets. I had to prove to the diving world and all sports fans that I was the same diver who had won the Commonwealth Games a few months before. I quickly found out that that's not exactly the way it works. I finished 17th. It was the worst experience so far in my life, but it has also turned out to be the best one for me.

After a few serious and honest conversations with Michel, my coach and great friend, I knew I had something to learn from this setback. I worried about what people would think of me now. Would they think that my win in Kuala Lumpur was just luck? That I was not a good diver after all? That I had not worked hard enough? That maybe I could not repeat my performance ever? Although I was very discouraged, I began to understand that I had not dived *for myself* but *against the others*.

Now I understand that I'm a human being after all, and that we all make mistakes. We also have to learn from these mistakes and that's what we call experience . . . real experience. I may be only 15 years old, but if that's the only thing I learn in my teen years, it will serve me all my life. Now and then that attitude comes back – that I am diving *against* other competitors, that I cannot fail because of what people will think – but I fight it. When I made it to the Olympics in 2000, I said to myself that I would once again dive for myself and have fun. For me, my fourth place at the Olympics was like a gold medal in my heart.

ALEXANDRE DESPATIE is a diver who was the youngest member of Canada's Team at the Olympic Games in Sydney, 2000. He was the youngest gold medallist in the history of the Commonwealth Games in Kuala Lumpur, 1998.

METODI IGOROV

In 1998, at the Commonwealth Games in Malaysia, I won the gold in my sport, pistol shooting. Second was an athlete from South Africa and when he saw my "pure" Canadian name – Igorov – he lodged a protest against me. He said I was not Canadian. Next day a committee checked my passport, citizenship, etc. Finally, I received my medal but by this time, all the newspapers had written about my story. I became so popular in Malaysia that two days later, when I was buying a dress for my wife, I got it at half price – the salesperson was reading an article about me, complete with picture, just at the time I was in his store. So sometimes it is not so bad to be a victim!

METODI IGOROV won the gold medal in Olympic Rapid Fire Pistol Shooting at the Commonwealth Games in Kuala Lumpur, 1998. He is a member of the Canadian Pistol Shooting Team and has been Canadian champion five times.

• 7 •

I OWE IT ALL TO . . .

I will always cherish the memory of my mum picking me up at lunchtime at Lonsdale Elementary School to hit with me at the nearby public tennis courts. I probably drove her nuts half the time, but we shared the joy of hitting the ball and I have her to thank for the wonderful lifestyle and experiences that I have enjoyed through tennis.

– Robert Bettauer, Canadian Tennis champion, Davis Cup player and Olympic coach

CURTIS JOSEPH

I 'd lived my whole life believing I'd never play in the NHL – I certainly didn't go through the regular routes of Triple A or the juniors – but I still harboured the dream. When I was at the University of Wisconsin, I played college hockey. NHL scouts came to our games and for some reason, I finally caught their eye. They started taking notice. One scout, David McNab, would send me handwritten letters of encouragement. The recognition that I was a good player started my dream rolling again and kept it alive. His interest – which was unusual, because scouts usually don't want to let you know they're there – motivated me to take the step of turning pro. I've always appreciated the extra effort he took, which gave me the confidence to believe I could pursue playing in the NHL. Sometimes the smallest gesture and one kind word can make a world of difference. It did for me.

CURTIS JOSEPH is a goaltender in the National Hockey League who played for the St. Louis Blues from 1989 to 1995, then was traded to the Edmonton Oilers in 1996. Since 1998 he has enjoyed a successful career with the Toronto Maple

Leafs. He was a member of Canada's Hockey Team at the Olympic Winter Games in Nagano, 1998.

ALWYN MORRIS

I have often been asked about that glorious day in August 1984. Not only was it the day my partner, Hugh Fisher, and I won Olympic gold, but it was the day I was able to make a special tribute to a person I valued, respected, and loved.

Many people have told me that that magical moment of stepping to the top of the podium was the conclusion of a momentous task. However, I always viewed the moment as a time to honour not only Canada, but also my cultural heritage as a Mohawk person.

I'm sure it was sometimes difficult for some of my kayaking teammates to fully understand who I really was. After all, they only saw the outside person, one who was an active, outgoing, and sometimes very stubborn and determined athlete. About a year before the 1984 Olympic Games, I decided to discuss with my teammates the idea I had about honouring my grandfather should we stand on the podium, and although they were supportive, they seemed somewhat perplexed.

I had grown up in an urban Indian reserve of Kahnawake just outside Montreal. As with most families during the late 1950s, family gatherings were commonplace. It was during those times that I found that my grandfather was more than just a grandpa, but rather a man who loved sports and was quite a proficient athlete himself. It was not hard to become closer and closer to him, and as time went on, I valued his advice about commitment, courage, respect, and determination. At the same time, I learned about my Mohawk cultural values and found that I was part of a unique heritage.

Unfortunately, my grandfather went to the spirit world long before I had my opportunity to compete at the Olympic Games. I now had to find solace in the messages and wisdom he had given me.

Over the next four years, I paddled thousands of kilometres in my quest to get to the Olympics. Still one unchangeable fact remained: My grandfather would never see me compete at the Games. I knew deep down, though, that he would be in Los Angeles in spirit, and I knew that I had to give him the recognition he deserved.

The difficult point for me was to decide what would be a fitting tribute to a man who meant so much to me. This dilemma went on for almost a year, and I know my teammates were getting somewhat worried that I would never find the appropriate symbol in time for the Games.

Often my grandfather said that things happen for a reason, and I guess my belief in that helped me in 1984. During our team's pre-Olympic camp in Sacramento, California, a group of urban aboriginal people visited our residence. I expressed an interest in attending one of their socials. During that social, I was honoured and presented with an eagle feather. Of course, the thrill of receiving the feather still stands out as a cherished moment in time, but the gesture also brought me back to my heritage. The eagle feather represents life, honour, and respect. I thought to myself, "How fitting," and wondered if this was the symbol I had been looking for. Always unsure of myself, I turned to the phone book. I knew that Billy Mills had been the second aboriginal person to win Olympic gold, the first one being Jim Thorpe. Not only had he won gold, but he lived in Sacramento! After some searching, I finally hit the jackpot. I had never met Billy Mills, and I was sure he wouldn't know who I was. Undaunted, I dialled his number. I introduced myself and explained my dilemma. I asked him about his experience growing up and how he felt having the opportunity to be in the Olympics as an aboriginal person. After our brief conversation, I decided I would honour my grandfather with the eagle feather I'd been honoured with.

In the end, I had the chance to share my Olympic experience, not only with other Mohawks, but with my grandfather when I raised the eagle feather as I stepped on top of the podium to accept my gold medal. As the sun shone on Hugh and me on that special day, I knew deep in my heart that my grandfather, and other aboriginal people around the world, were sharing that connection with me.

I still talk to Billy Mills and, yes, the eagle feather adorns a special place in my home. To this day, I cannot help but think that my grandfather is still with me and the feather helps to keep us together.

ALWYN MORRIS was the gold medallist and bronze medallist in Kayak at the Olympic Games in Los Angeles, 1984, and a member of the Canadian Olympic Team in Seoul, 1988.

DANIEL IGALI

I was born in Bayelsa State in the southeastern part of Nigeria, Africa, where I started wrestling at a very young age. It was the only sport apart from soccer that I did as a kid. My tribesmen, the Ijaw clansmen, are noted for their skill in wrestling. I was told that my grandfather did not pay a bride prize for my grandmother because he was a village wrestling champion – that is how wrestlers were valued in those days in my tribe. As a youth, I wanted to be a village wrestling champion. All my idols were great wrestlers from my village (Eniwari) and other neighbouring villages. Even though wrestling was a great pastime, there had never been any wrestler from my tribe or even Africa who had won a gold medal at the World Championship and Olympic level. The traditional style of wrestling did not embody freestyle rules – in traditional wrestling, a takedown was an automatic win, but in freestyle you wrestled for six minutes and were awarded points for different holds, including takedowns. I wanted to be a good wrestler, and when I was at the Commonwealth Games in Victoria in 1994, I could see that in Canada there would be many opportunities to improve myself – there were good coaches, excellent facilities, and more tournaments to compete at. I decided to stay in Canada and worked with the Immigration Department to be able to stay here.

With a little bag containing a few clothes and about $500, I decided come rain or shine, I was going to tough it out in this new land. If I was going to be any good (I had placed 11th at the Commonwealth Games), I thought Canada was the place to try it and nothing was going to stop me.

The Olympic Games in Sydney are around the corner. We are camped in Mittagong, a little city about 100 kilometres south of Sydney, preparing for the Olympic showdown. Strangely, the birds chirp all evening and are the first to wake me up in the morning. They are singing me the coronation song ahead of time.

Twice in the last two days, I have seen her in my dreams. In one she is lying down and in a barely audible voice, she tells me she thinks she will make it to the tournament. The second time I see her she has a cloth tied around her chest, in traditional Ijaw fashion, which signifies support for a child or loved one. A child is normally tightly strapped around the mother's back for safety. In effect, she was telling me that she was going all the way with me.

She walks into my room without knocking and opens her arms as if she wants a hug. It is customary for us to hug, but this time, I am reluctant. In fact, I do not want to hug her. After a few minutes, she sits down on the sofa across from me. We stare at each other for a few minutes before she tells me she is very proud of me. She is very familiar, but I cannot bring myself to recognize her. I tell her "Thank you." It is the only thing I know how to say these days. I wake up from my dream and realize then that she is Maureen Matheny, my surrogate mother in Canada who had died five days after I won the World Championships in 1999. She had fallen ill before the championships with a deadly form of cancer but had promised me she would go to the Olympics. "We are going to beat this thing," she had said, but she had died just after my success.

I had woken up all sweaty and invigorated. It was less than two hours from the finals of the wrestling competition. I remembered the last words she had said to me in her deathbed when I came back from the championships in 1999: "I am very proud of you." With that realization, I thanked God for giving my angel a day pass to watch over her adopted son. Just as she had promised back in 1999, she made it to the Olympics. I did not have any reason to doubt her because she had never broken a promise. Even in death, she was at the Olympics to support her warrior. Who says there are no guardian angels?

DANIEL IGALI was the gold medallist in Freestyle Wrestling at the Olympic Games in Sydney, 2000, and was also the Freestyle Wrestling World Wrestling Champion. He was named Canada's Athlete of the Year for 1999 and 2000.

ALEC J. DENYS

I will always remember the first time I met Gerry Bryant. I was in my second month of rehab at the Kingston General Hospital. I had suffered a spinal cord injury when I fell from a tree while bowhunting on November 25, 1979. After surgery and a month of treatment to stabilize my condition, I was now in the middle of intensive rehabilitation to learn, at the age of 29, new life skills as a paraplegic.

The Saturday morning that Gerry showed up was just another day of gruelling physiotherapy and mind-numbing boredom. I was a long way from coming to terms with my situation.

I was in my room when a short bald person with a very pronounced limp (Gerry had had polio) walked in and almost commanded, "Come on! Let's go play some basketball." He left without waiting for a reply.

Who was this guy? Hadn't he noticed I was in a body cast from chin to hips and was sitting in a wheelchair? How was I supposed to play basketball? The old fool!

I couldn't believe what had happened. I just had to find out where this guy was coming from. When I arrived at the gym, the five other patients in rehab were there as well. Gerry had brought along a half dozen lightweight wheelchairs, and in a matter of minutes we were all doing drills and learning the game of wheelchair basketball.

By spring I had shed the cast and a huge amount of self-pity and was playing with the Kingston Wheelies, the wheelchair basketball team Gerry coached and played with.

While Gerry was very supportive and encouraging, he would not tolerate giving up. He coached by example, never letting his disability be an excuse. If it wasn't possible to do something a certain way because of the disability, he found a way around it that had the same result.

Gerry also encouraged me to train for the upcoming Eastern Ontario Regional Games for the Physically Disabled. He showed me the fine points of throwing javelin, shot put, and discus, bench-pressing weights, and wheelchair racing. Those first games in Cornwall were amazing for me and started the rebuilding of my confidence and self-esteem.

My interest and success in sport for the disabled grew quickly under Gerry's guidance and I was soon competing at provincial and national levels. I developed a tremendous respect and friendship with this little "old" bald guy who never let me focus on my disability but only on ability and potential.

Gerry died only a few years after that day in February when he had walked into my room but I have carried the image and spirit of Gerry with me to the many Paralympic Games I have competed in. His legacy continues in me and in the future Paralympians I hope to inspire.

ALEC J. DENYS is an archer who represented Canada at the Paralympic Games in Sydney, 2000. He has been a member of the Canadian Paralympic Team since 1984.

SYLVIA BURKA

The jubilant announcer kept repeating in Norwegian that I was the new 1976 World Champion in speed skating. As I skated through the corner where my parents were standing, I stopped in front of them and kept repeating deliriously, "I've won! I've won!" My legs were exhausted from the effort, so I was bent over bracing my hands on my legs, tears of joy running down my cheeks. My parents just stood there and stared at me with care and compassion, unsure of how to comfort me. They couldn't figure out why I was saying "I've won" when there was no doubt that I had been clearly beaten by the person I had been paired with. It took a few moments for the pieces to fall into place – she had beaten me in this race but my overall point total for the four races meant I was the champion – and finally the announcer repeated in English that I was the new World Champion.

As my parents slowly realized that I had finally fulfilled my dream, their look of concern turned to jubilation.

We always hear about the sacrifices that the athletes make to reach the top but I think the sacrifices the parents make are much greater. Parents support you in the good times and in the bad times, and win or lose, they are still your biggest fans.

SYLVIA BURKA was the World Speed Skating Champion in 1976 and the World Sprint Champion in 1977. She was a member of Canada's Olympic Team at the Olympic Winter Games in Sapporo, 1972, Innsbruck, 1976, and Lake Placid, 1980.

CURTIS HIBBERT

When I was three, my family and I – I had six older brothers and sisters – left Jamaica and moved to Canada. Canada was a wonderful place where, with a little hard work, there were lots of opportunities. Everyone was so busy starting a new life in Toronto that no one had much time to notice my new best friend, television. I would sit and watch for hours. Soon, though, my family caught on and decided it was time to get me outside into the real world – a world where my head could be challenged, a world where my body could move – the world of sports. They put me in soccer, in basketball, in baseball, in swimming, in everything! Where all my brothers and sisters succeeded, I failed at every single one of them. So they said, with little hope, "Okay, one last chance, let's try him in gymnastics." I was seven. It was the start of a dream. And I owe it all to TV.

CURTIS HIBBERT is a gymnast who represented Canada at the Olympic Games in Seoul, 1988, and in Barcelona, 1992.

He was a silver medallist in 1987 and a bronze medallist in 1992 at the World Gymnastic Championships. He was the first Canadian to win a World Championship medal in Gymnastics.

HAYLEY WICKENHEISER

I grew up in a small town, Shaunavon, Saskatchewan, population 2,000. Sports were a big part of my life. My parents are teachers and were heavily involved with local activities at the rink – my mum curled and my dad played hockey. It was only natural that my younger brother and sister and I should grow up as rink rats. I especially loved hockey. I would play hockey in the winter and then throw my skates in the closet and pick up a ball glove to pay softball in the summer. When ball season ended, I couldn't wait to lace my skates up again.

My parents didn't push me. They simply said, "We don't care what you do but you must do something. You must be active." One of the greatest things they understood when I was a kid was the power of a dream. When I was 10, in 1988, my mum and dad took us to Calgary, a five-hour drive, to be part of the Winter Olympic Games. We got to see only one event, ski jumping, because tickets were so expensive. It didn't really matter. What mattered was that we had the chance to be there, to experience the atmosphere and the Olympic spirit. We were on top of the world.

My parents took us to a mall to go shopping. A little kiosk was set up selling Olympic paraphernalia. I found a poster that I just loved. It was a collage showing all the sports, countries, flags, and venues – the title was "Calgary '88." The price was

$50, which was far too expensive for what it was really worth. But price didn't matter. Despite my parents telling me not to, I bought the poster, along with pins and T-shirts and anything else Olympic I could afford. To this day, I have that poster on my wall. It's a little tattered and a little faded but it means so much to me. It symbolized the beginning of my own Olympic dream. Being able to go to Calgary and see the Olympics firsthand inspired me. As small-town kids, we did not have the opportunity to see events like this very often. The Olympics had seemed worlds away from the world I grew up in, until I went to Calgary. In Calgary, I saw how regular people volunteered their time to put the games on. I also saw and felt the impact of the Olympic spirit and the tension of competition. I knew it was where I belonged.

HAYLEY WICKENHEISER was a silver medallist on Canada's Women's Ice Hockey Team, Olympic Winter Games in Nagano, 1998. She was also a member of Canada's Softball Team at the Olympic Games in Sydney, 2000. She has been on four gold medal teams for Canada at the World Championships in Ice Hockey and has received the Bruce Kidd Award for Athlete Leadership.

LISA LING

My dad, a karate expert, taught my sisters and me karate. He taught us how to punch and kick not long after we learned how to walk and talk and chew solid food. It wasn't always smooth sailing. I wanted to quit karate many times. Occasionally my sisters and I ganged up on Dad. But before we mustered the courage to face our father, we went to our mother.

"Mum, we all want to quit karate. It's too hard and we don't like it anymore," my eldest sister would say with a determined look on her face.

"Okay, okay," Mum would reply. "Just get changed into your gis (our karate clothing), and go downstairs. Dad's waiting for you. I'll bake you some cookies and they'll be ready for you by the time you're finished your workout." At her simple bribe and show of solidarity with Dad, we'd reluctantly trudge downstairs, line up in age order, bow in, and begin training. Quitting was simply not an option. Now at 29 I am the nine-time Canadian karate champion and all because of cookies!

LISA LING was a bronze medallist in Karate at the Pan American Games in Winnipeg, 1999, and World Soke Cup Karate Champion. She is a nine-time Canadian Karate champion.

• 8 •

UNFORGETTABLE

I won't ever forget the last day of the Games in Nagano. Cross-country skier Guido Visser finished last in the 50-kilometre race — the last athlete to enter the stadium in the last event of the Games. Seventeen skiers abandoned the race, but not him. Anyone who watched the cross-country skiing saw the terrible snow and miserable weather. And, when others dropped out, rather than finish in the back of the pack in these awful conditions, Guido Visser refused to give up. All he had to do to keep going, he said, was think about the people at home who believed in him and who were up in the middle of the night watching him on TV.

— Alain Guilbert, writing about Guido Visser, member of Canada's Cross-Country Ski Team, Olympic Winter Games, Nagano, 1998

DEBBI WILKES

The 1964 Olympic Winter Games in Innsbruck, Austria, featured competition nestled beneath the peaks of the spectacular Tyrolean Mountains. Unlike the Games today, the Winter Olympics then were still held on a relatively small scale with only 36 countries and 1,100 athletes participating.

Apart from the ice arena, which hosted hockey and figure skating inside and speed skating outside, the venues were small and practical. Although the rink was large, tickets to events only bought you "space," not a seat. The stands consisted of wide concrete stairs with a metal counter sticking up every ten feet or so. By leaning on it, you could watch the event . . . *and* eat the most amazing Wiener schnitzel!

Other sites were great for competing but less than "friendly" for the fans. At the Opening Ceremonies held outdoors at the ski jumping venue, family, friends, and fans practically had to scale the side of the mountain to beg for a seat in the stadium. Even if you held a ticket, the capacity was so tiny, there were no guarantees you'd be admitted.

Problems getting in, yes. But once there, visitors had a breathtaking view. Huge, craggy, snow-covered mountains rose up to the skies with a sense of majesty that made a powerful statement; the sound was so quiet and pure, everyone spoke with a whisper.

Even the ski jumpers treated the scene with respect . . . although ironically, not because of the mountain view. From the top of the jump, they could see beyond the bowl into a more earthly example of nature, a symbol of the crazy risk they took with every jump above the Tyrol. Carved into the side of the mountain was an enormous graveyard.

DEBBI WILKES was Canadian and North American Pairs Figure Skating champion and silver medallist with her partner Guy Revell at the Olympic Winter Games in Innsbruck, 1964. The team was recently inducted into the Canadian Figure Skating Hall of Fame.

CHRIS WIGHTMAN

There are two things I will never forget about Sarajevo. The first is how extraordinary a city it was. The second is that I have never been more scared in my life.

My first trip to Sarajevo was in December 1986 for a Luge World Cup race. It was halfway through my third season on the Canadian Luge Team. My rookie season had been as a wide-eyed junior and my second as a quick-learning senior. I had to learn quickly because I had no other choice.

In the sport of luge, junior men start lower on track than senior men, but at the same start as the women and doubles. At the beginning of my second season, when I turned senior, the coaches suggested that I compete in doubles, partly because I had the right tall and thin build for it but also so that I could stay at the lower start and learn the European tracks more gradually. I agreed, but less than a month into that second season my doubles partner had a nasty crash and injured his neck badly during training.

Later that night when the coaches returned from the hospital, they told me that our season as a doubles team was over but that I had a choice – I could either go home or continue to slide singles. It didn't take long to figure out which of the choices was going to eliminate any chance of fulfilling my dream of getting to the Olympics. So I went to the top with the big boys and paid my dues. By the next season everything was going much better because I had raced at all of the tracks – all, that is, except Sarajevo.

Sarajevo was still showing signs of glory from hosting the winter Olympics three years previously. After travelling by bus for 24 hours from our last race in Germany, we drove briefly through the city centre and saw some of the Olympic facilities and colourful banners hanging from the lightposts.

While most luge tracks are located near small ski resort towns, Sarajevo was the only track other than Calgary and Innsbruck that was near a major city. It was a refreshing change to see the hustle and bustle of a big city. Even from my seat on the bus I knew I was going to like this place. I couldn't wait to get out and look around. But the bus headed out of town and dropped us at our hotel about 10 kilometres further into the surrounding hills. We stopped and checked into our hotel. It was a popular spot about halfway between downtown and the luge track. The friendly and energetic staff quickly fed us and got us settled in our rooms. At last, a real bed and not a bus seat.

The next morning after a delicious breakfast complete with strong Turkish coffee, we continued up the hillside road to the track. When we got off the bus, the first thing I noticed was the spectacular view we had of Sarajevo, nestled in a picturesque snow-capped mountain valley. This place was growing on me by the second.

As always, upon arriving at a new track, we walked the length of it, getting the lay of the land, memorizing the combination of curves and getting instructions from the coaches about the best way to take each curve and approximately where to steer. It was clear this track was going to be fast, and it looked like one that I should do well on. The long straight-aways and big curves were similar to our home track in Calgary. But by the time our first training runs were scheduled to start later that day, a thick fog had rolled into the valley and the session was cancelled. It was the thickest fog I had ever been in – you could barely see the end of your outstretched arm. With many days to go before the race, the coaches suggested we go downtown, below the fog, to do some sightseeing in case we couldn't go later on.

The bus dropped me and my teammates off in the middle of the city and we quickly headed off in our own directions. To my surprise, I turned the first corner only to realize that I was at the infamous site of the assassination of Austro-Hungary's Archduke Ferdinand, an act that triggered the First World War. It was sort of like stumbling through Dallas and unexpectedly being sandwiched between the Texas School Book Depository and a grassy knoll. I soaked up the information on the multilingual plaque and continued wandering down the busy streets.

In the heart of the business district, murals of Yugoslavia's leader, General Tito, graced the sides of buildings and national flags waved proudly in classic communist style. But nearby in huge indoor marketplaces, like so many cities in Europe, farmers and locals bartered across the well-stocked counters for their fresh daily produce. Further along, in an old warehouse, a flea market was bustling with local hustlers hawking their trinkets. Just down a side street I hooked up with some of my teammates and checked out the nearby artisan studios whose doors were bursting with objects that had a distinct Turkish flair.

As the evening darkness settled over the city, I could hear the sound of church bells ringing in the distance, but I also heard something I had never heard before – a wailing voice being broadcast to the neighbourhood. I turned off the main avenue to see where it was coming from. I quickly came upon its source and function, a loudspeaker high above the courtyard of a magnificent mosque calling Sarajevo's Muslim population to prayer. I had never seen a mosque before and I had certainly never heard chanting like this, echoing off the downtown office buildings. Fascinated, I stopped outside the gates and peered in to watch the hundreds of men on their knees praying in orderly rows.

While elements of Sarajevo had a European familiarity, other elements were just the opposite. It was magnificent. It was like a crossroads of culture and for the first time in ages my senses were alive. It was one of the greatest cities I had ever been to. People dressed with class and cosmopolitan flair. There was something interesting around almost every corner. The abundance of diesel exhaust even gave it a distinct smell.

The food was great, and the Sarajevans' *joie de vivre* lasted well into the night as I lay in my bed that night listening to the dull heartbeat of the disco in the basement of our hotel.

The fog that had rolled into the valley a day earlier didn't seem to want to leave. Our training runs were cancelled almost every day. Never having been to this track, I desperately needed to get as many training runs in before the race as possible. At least three or four, and preferably more. In the end I only got two, both starting lower on the track, which is customary so you can gradually build up to the track's top velocity.

At the end of that second and last training run I was still having problems in the middle section of the track, flying off the ends of a few successive curves and being slammed into the adjoining walls. I was out of control. Going faster, from farther up the track, without fixing the present problems was just going to throw me harder into the walls and who knew what else. I couldn't believe my ears when they cancelled the final training session. It left me with the emptiest feeling I have ever experienced. I was scared, mainly because in this sport of centimetres, there were about 100 metres of track I had never been on. For the first time since I started sliding I didn't know what lay ahead of me. It was like I was about to jump out of a plane not knowing how to open the chute.

That night I couldn't sleep. The unfamiliarity of this city, which I loved so much a few days before, I now hated. I didn't want to be there.

The next morning, the fog had cleared just enough for us to race, but it was by no means gone. When we got to the track I took my sled and equipment into the start hut. I went to the top of the start ramp and looked out. I needed to visualize what I had to do in this upper and still unknown part of the track. I was hoping to be able to see the spot, a few curves further down the track, where I had started my last training run. Instead what I saw was a wall of fog. I couldn't see the first curve. I couldn't even see the bottom of the steep start ramp. I had never felt as helpless and alone in my life.

After the initial anxiety attack passed, I knew I had to focus. The only way out of the situation was to take it into my own hands, and to use the skills I had to make it work.

"The track is clear for Chris Wightman from Canada," barked the race announcer in broken English. The green light flicked on and I had 30 seconds to push off.

I wouldn't say that my life flashed in front of my eyes, but it was one of those moments when your mind rushes so fast, you have a hundred thoughts a second. Everything was hyper-real, the ice was whiter than it had ever been, the beautiful tall pines around the track were greener than ever and my heart was beating louder than ever. And then it happened, just as it did at the beginning of every other race: the long hours of training paid off as my mind and body met and did what they were supposed to do – race.

If anything, my pull form from the start handles was stronger than normal with all of the extra anxiety and adrenaline pumping through my body. As I lay down on my sled, I improvised my way through the first few unknown curves. Then everything started looking familiar again, coming at me a little bit faster, but at least familiar. It wasn't a perfect run, but it was better than the last and when I got off my sled at the bottom I couldn't wait to go back to the top. Finally it was fun again.

I learned a lot in Sarajevo. I learned a lot about myself and I realized that I was in the position I was in because I had the skills to get myself through it. I have used that experience many times since. Just because you don't know what exactly is ahead, just believe in yourself and you'll get through it.

I also learned about a new country, one that was different but at the same time familiar. I say familiar because Yugoslavia, at that time, was similar to Canada with several different ethnic groups living in relative peace and harmony. Sarajevo showcased it. The important lesson was that the mix of diverse cultures made it really interesting and gave it an extra dimension. It made me stop and notice, it made me feel alive, and it left me wanting to go back.

I did go back, the next year, for another World Cup in which I did much better. Every day I couldn't wait to finish training so I could go and explore the streets of Sarajevo. It was the only place on the tour where I really wanted to do that.

But now I don't know if I could go back.

The luge and bobsled track is decimated, full of gaping wounds from mortar shells. During the war, its fifteen-foot-high, two-foot-thick concrete walls served as a serpentine bunker, housing deadly artillery high in the hills overlooking Sarajevo. I have heard it became, ironically, somewhat of a graveyard too. With each direct hit from enemy guns, the ammonia-filled refrigeration pipes embedded in the track exploded, releasing toxic gas on the unsuspecting sentries.

Our wonderful hotel halfway up the hill is also gone. All of the great hospitality and the heartbeat of the disco snuffed out by whatever faction claimed it as theirs.

And I'll never forget the horror of watching television news reports about the bloody bombings on the markets in downtown Sarajevo that I loved so much. Innocent people gathering food for their day, blown up by the cowardly guns on the surrounding hills.

I often think of all the people I met in Sarajevo who were so glad to have international athletes in town. The artisans, the shopkeepers, our waiter who made us laugh every day.

I know the fear I felt during that race was nothing compared to the horror Sarajevans went through day in and day out for almost four years.

I wonder how they made out during the war; I wonder if they are alive or dead. I am so glad that I saw Sarajevo when I did. After all the Olympic crowds had left and before all the hatred took over.

I wonder if Sarajevo will ever be like that again.

CHRIS WIGHTMAN was a member of Canada's Luge Team in the Olympic Winter Games in Calgary, 1988, and competed for Canada in the World Championships in Innsbruck, 1987.

MONIQUE KAVELAARS

For most athletes, myself included, the Olympic Games represent the pinnacle of one's athletic achievement. It would be easy to assume that we all face similar struggles getting there. This is not the case.

When you're an athlete competing at the international level, you get to see the entire world and make friends from all over. Over the years, you become familiar with the other athletes who you see from tournament to tournament. Some you get to know, trading stories and catching up on each other's lives. With others, because of a language barrier, you might simply acknowledge each other with a smile. In any case, you meet many different people, all with very different life experiences. For a few years, I would always see this one woman from Yugoslavia – she was a very intense fencer.

She would often show up at tournaments close to her home – Hungary, Slovakia, and Poland. Five years ago, she had a baby but returned to competition soon after. Her father, who was also her coach, would look after the baby during competitions. It has always inspired me to see women competing after having had children.

All athletes eventually retire to pursue other goals, jobs, and responsibilities, so when someone drops out of the scene, you usually assume they've moved on. But about two years ago when I realized I hadn't seen her in quite some time, I wondered if she was all right. She was from Bosnia, and we were all aware of the situation in Yugoslavia. Being from Canada, most of what I knew I had learned from newspapers and television reports. This was the first time something that seemed so far away and frightening had come so close. There was a face. There was a name.

It took my breath away in the spring of 2000 to see her walk into the gym in Budapest at our last World Cup to qualify for Sydney. Still accompanied by her father, she looked thinner and her uniform, the same one she had worn two years ago, was grey and worn.

Her chances of qualifying for Sydney were a long shot. But, man, did she look determined! Her having shown up in Budapest was impressive enough. None of us knew what the last two years had been like for her. I can only assume training had been near impossible. We were able to speak about it briefly, and she explained how difficult life had been for her and her family, but she was looking forward to competing next month at the "winner takes all" European Zonal Competition. You win it – you qualify for the Olympics! I was happy to see her back. She competed well in Budapest, but winning next month's competition seemed like a rather unrealistic goal, given how long she had been off the scene.

Not having qualified for Sydney, I returned home to Canada to my training routine and to prepare for Nationals. A month later I went online to see how the European Zonal Comp. had unfolded. I knew it would be a tough one. There were some strong fencers, many of them friends of mine, competing for the single qualifying spot. I was shocked and pleased to see that she had won the whole thing!

Although I wasn't attending the Sydney Olympics as an athlete, I was fortunate to be there on behalf of the Toronto 2008 Olympic Bid. Being there was incredible, watching different events, meeting people from all over the world again, but watching the fencing was a special treat. I saw my friend from Yugoslavia compete. She was fencing with the strongest desire I'd ever seen. She made it through to the round before the final 16 and was up against the former Olympic champion. She lost in the end, but she gave the French girl a run for her money!

It struck me that my own struggle to qualify had been so different from hers, and I began to wonder about the other journeys people had taken to get here, difficult journeys I will never know about. If medals could be awarded for persevering against insurmountable odds, then my Bosnian friend would be a contender for the gold.

MONIQUE KAVELAARS is a fencer who won a silver medal in the team event at the Pan American Games in Winnipeg, 1999. She is currently competing to qualify for the Olympic Games in Athens, 2004.

BILL CROTHERS

During my years of competitive racing, I had the opportunity to visit almost 20 different countries, on all continents except South America. I still cherish memories from those times. I can remember watching lineups of people being given vaccinations with a common needle sterilized between uses in a Bunsen flame in an African country and then being told I had to have a yellow fever inoculation. I remember competing in Eastern Europe where there were no showers and having to share a bathtub with a Yugoslavian shot putter. I can remember handing out flowers, with a teammate, to women on the main street of downtown Budapest – just because we thought it would be fun to do.

BILL CROTHERS was the silver medallist in the 800 metres in Track and Field at the Olympic Games in Tokyo, 1964. He was ranked number one in the world in his event in 1965.

· 9 ·

WHY NOT ME?

Why couldn't I compete at age 34? In February 1995, I quit my job, packed my bags, and moved to Winnipeg for 15 months of full-time training to qualify for my second Olympics. I became the second oldest player to compete in the Women's Volleyball competition at the 1996 Olympic Games. If you want to live your life with no regrets, you have to do things that are not always comfortable and convenient.

– Diane Ratnik, member of Canada's Volleyball Team, Olympic Games, Los Angeles, 1984, and Atlanta, 1996

MARK TEWKSBURY

*W**hy not me?*

Such a simple question. Yet it would forever change my life.

Lying on my single bed in the minuscule room I shared with another athlete in the Olympic Village, with the blinds drawn to escape the blazing sun if not the suffocating heat for a while, I realized what this moment held for me. My dream was so close – for fleeting moments I could feel it, I could see it. But then it was gone. There was still one last obstacle to overcome. And I was very afraid.

I had waited what seemed an eternity for this opportunity, and now it was finally here. Well, almost. Sixteen years ago this journey had begun and now I only had to wait another five hours. After coming all this way, I knew only too well it could be these last hours that would do me in.

That morning I had gone to the Olympic swimming pool with a clear objective in mind. The Olympic swimming competition is a two-part affair. The best 75 men in the world in the 100-metre backstroke come together for the morning heats where, following 30 minutes of competition, 67 of us find ourselves eliminated. Although we spoke different languages, worshipped different gods, and represented different cultures, on this day we all shared two common goals: We wanted to be our best, and we did not want to be one of those eliminated 67.

I had a breakthrough swim that morning, registering a personal best, a Canadian and Commonwealth record, and had placed second among my competitors. For a moment I could breathe a sigh of relief – but only for a moment. The real test was still to come.

This was not the first time I had qualified for an Olympic final. In Seoul, four years earlier, I had qualified for the final of the 100-metre backstroke, albeit in seventh place. I had entered the Olympics a medal favourite, but during the Games I had been plagued by intense feelings of inadequacy. In all the details that had gone into my preparation, I had overlooked how I would feel being surrounded by the world's best athletes, day in and day out. I had assumed that things would take care of themselves; that the magic that had propelled me to be one of the best in the world at what I did would appear as always. I kept waiting for it to come. But it never did. Instead, my own thoughts began to betray me, keeping me awake at night thinking of what I should have done but had not. I wondered if I was as good as those around me. I questioned how I ever got here in the first place. I would lie awake at night paralyzed by fear. Nobody had to beat me in Seoul; I had already beaten myself.

So here I was, four years later, with only hours separating another Olympic final and myself, alone with my thoughts. Many things went through my mind. I remembered the coaches who had taught me along the way – all of them! –

and how out of the thousands of swimmers that had crossed my path through the years, somehow *I* had ended up here. I thought of how incredible Jeff Rouse, the world record holder from America, had looked that morning as he won his heat. I thought of the Spanish crowd that would fill the 10,000-seat stadium that evening and cheer for Martín López-Zubero, the gold medallist in the 200. I thought of my parents, who were somewhere in Barcelona right now. And then I thought of the scoreboard after the last heat and how four of us were within three-tenths of a second going into the final. And that scared me.

One of us was going to be fourth tonight. I did not want that to be me. I wanted a medal so much . . . I had come so far. Instead of running away from it, I faced the fear. I seriously contemplated coming fourth. Then third. Funny, but neither felt right. So I pushed on. I thought of placing second. Again, something about it did not feel right.

I sat up in my bed, took a deep, deep breath, and dared to think clearly what had for so long been but a foggy dream. With all the energy and focus I could muster, I imagined myself coming first. Probably because I had never won at a competition like this before, it felt strange. But then, from somewhere deep inside me a voice, very faint at first, asked a question. "*Why not me?*" Then silence. Where I would usually find a barrage of excuses, none came. Except the voice again, but this time a little bit louder. "*Why not me?*" Again, silence. I felt my shoulders lower. I inhaled and exhaled deeply.

"Somebody has to win the race tonight. Why not me?"

All the fear, all the self-doubt that I had carried for so long, all the pressure was lifted. Gone. I felt completely at peace. I cried for a moment. I imagine it was the final letting go of whatever barrier was holding me back from realizing my potential. And in that moment I knew that it didn't matter if I won the race or not. No matter what happened, at least I had not beaten myself.

MARK TEWKSBURY is a swimmer who was a gold and bronze medallist at the Olympic Games in Barcelona, 1992. He was a silver medallist at the Olympic Games in Seoul, 1988.

REBECCAH BORNEMANN

I remember when I was trapped inside a body that didn't work, and couldn't get out. I'd figured out that I was different from the other kids – for one thing, they didn't have to go to physiotherapy – but I didn't fully understand what the implications of that difference were. All I knew was the frustration of trying to organize my feet to dribble the soccer ball, of trying to connect the badminton racquet to the birdie, of not being able to accomplish what my classmates seemed to achieve, if not effortlessly, easily. By the time I'd learn to serve, my classmates were playing new games. I'd practise with my dad in the evenings, but progress was agonizingly slow. Cerebral palsy had its challenges.

A couple of years and many false starts later, I found myself standing on the pool deck on a Wednesday evening. I had reluctantly agreed to try a disability swimming program, just one time. I'd loved swimming once, had been upset when casts on my legs meant missing a session of lessons, and had struggled my way through all the Red Cross badges.

Now, after swimming up and down the length of the pool, I was surprised when the coach said, "You're good, and you're coming back next week, right?" I don't think I was convinced, but some positive feedback was better than none, and I soon learned once again to enjoy swimming.

I loved being able to chart my progress in the pool. I could swim farther in each practice, and I could swim the lengths faster against the clock. When we went away to a competition, I saw that not only were there other people who had disabilities like me, but that I could swim as well as they could, even better. Sue, my coach, was pleased with my progress, even proud. Within a couple of years, my times had improved dramatically.

In 1988, a friend who came to the pool for cross-training made the Canadian track team for the Seoul Paralympic Games. It was the first time I'd heard of the Paralympics, but seeing Jamie's hard work and intensive training, I knew it had to be a big deal. In September, I watched the Olympics on television, to see where he would be going. In October, I scoured the newspaper for word of his results. Gold medals. World records. I was entranced and hooked. For the first time, I dreamed I might achieve something like that too.

The next year I made the national team. I started university and trained with the school swim team. When I received word I'd made the team for the 1992 Barcelona Paralympic Games, I could hardly believe my good fortune. I really wanted to win a medal but didn't dare say it aloud. I wanted my results to be worthy not only of my own hard work, but of the support that others – coaches, family, friends – had given me.

In Barcelona, the stands at the pool were filled to capacity, and the waiting crowd spilled out into the street. This was it, *the* Paralympic Games, our opportunity to show the world what we could do.

I can remember clearly what it was like to sit in the ready room before my first race, my big race, feeling my stomach flip-flop. The world record was almost broken in the first heat by an Australian girl no one had heard of before. What on earth was I doing here? No way could I swim that fast. Impossible. Stunned, I went out on deck, desperately trying to pull myself together. Finally the training kicked in, and the familiar motions of getting on the blocks, diving in, and swimming took over. I swam and swam and swam, for what felt like an eternity. My hands and feet were blocks of ice, and I wasn't at all certain when I reached the end of the 400 metres. In terror I looked at the clock, convinced that I'd blown my chances. Instead, against all odds (still far off the world record mark), I'd swum a personal best for the 400. And I had qualified for the finals!

That night I was calmer, more focused. I was still dazed, but more in control of my thoughts. The thousands-strong audience was bigger than anything I'd ever imagined, but they shrank away as I looked down the length of the pool. Me and my lane – it was my race to lose.

At the end of the evening I stood on the podium watching the German, Australian, and Canadian flags run up the flagpole, a bronze medal around my neck. At that moment, I felt free. I had achieved my goals, and I had justified the faith and support that others had given me. It was as though a door had been opened into a country I had never imagined. On the other side of the impossible lay a whole world of possibilities.

REBECCAH BORNEMANN was a gold medallist for Canada in Swimming at the Paralympic Games, in Atlanta, 1996, and won two bronze medals at the Paralympic Games in Barcelona, 1992.

EVA-MARIA PRACHT

I was walking down the street in Toronto on a summer evening in 1987 when I thought it would be fun to let one of the Gypsy ladies read my palm. She looked into my eyes, took my hand, and told me I would be going on a faraway trip in the summer of 1988. She could see me wearing something shiny around my neck, such as a medal, an award of some kind. She said, "I don't know exactly what it is but it's a huge honour and very, very special."

Oh my god, I thought, the Olympic Games in Seoul, Korea, will be held during the summer of 1988! At that time I was shortlisted for the equestrian sport of discipline dressage. Canada had never won an Olympic medal in dressage.

A year later as I was bending down to receive my bronze medal, I suddenly remembered my experience with the Gypsy and immediately was covered with goosebumps. I wished I could have shared my happiness with her, but I never saw her again.

EVA-MARIA PRACHT was a member of Canada's Equestrian Dressage Team that won a bronze medal at the Olympic Games in Seoul, 1988. She was also on the Olympic Team in

Los Angeles, 1984, and won a gold medal at the Pan American Games in Indianapolis, 1987.

GORD TUCK

When I was 18, my life took a new direction when I was working in the forestry industry. I was crushed by a machine and thanks to the fast work of my co-workers and the skill of the doctors, I did not lose both legs – just one.

Nine years later I can do everything I used to do, some things even better. I have learned not to think of myself as a disabled person, but as an athlete with a visible disability. Everyone has some sort of disability they must overcome, it's just that for some people it may be more visible.

I have also learned the hard way over the years not to ever give up. In a World Cup Giant Slalom race a few years ago, I felt like I was struggling throughout my run, fighting the course all the way down. Three-quarters of the way down, I gave up and skied off to the side of the course. One of the U.S. ski team coaches came over to me and asked, "What are you doing?" I replied, "It just felt terrible, I was tired of fighting it." He said, "That's too bad, you were the fastest racer down the course up until here." From that day on, I decided no matter what, don't give up until after you cross the finish line!

GORD TUCK is a Canadian Disabled Alpine Ski Team member who represented Canada at the Paralympic Winter Games in Nagano, 1998. He was the Downhill silver medallist at the World Championships and is the current Canadian Downhill, Giant Slalom, and Slalom champion.

PAT REID

In 1967, when I was 20 years old and in my last year of the four-year Honours Physical Education program at the University of Western Ontario, the curling team I was on won the Ontario-Quebec Universities Championship. This win gave us the right to represent Ontario in the Canadian Olympiad in Calgary in March of 1967, part of a number of special Canadian events set up to celebrate Centennial Year. My teammates and I prepared for this national challenge and were pretty excited when we got on that plane to Calgary. For some of us, it was the first time we had ever been on a plane.

The competition was a round-robin format with no playoff – the top team after the competition would be the winner unless there was a tie, in which case a tiebreaker game would be played. As the luck of the draw had it, we were scheduled to play against Saskatchewan in the final draw. Although we had had a good week and won all our games leading into that final draw, the Saskatchewan team had played really well also and had won all their games, setting the stage for what was essentially a championship game in the final draw.

The comparison between teams ended there. We were undefeated but a few of our games were close, we won a game or two by good luck when opponents missed shots that would have made them the winners, and we won a few quite handily.

Saskatchewan, on the other hand, had been an awesome force all week long, dominating their opponents and winning every game by huge scores. They were an experienced team, whereas we were friends who had put a rink together for the year. They were a team who calculated where to roll the stone after a hit – we concentrated on just making the hit. They had an experienced coach, we had a chaperone. Like all the other competitors, I was in awe of their talent.

The night before the final draw to determine the Canadian championship, we had a meeting to talk about the upcoming game. We wanted to give Saskatchewan a good game and did not want to be blown away, so we resolved to keep it open and simple and try to stay with them as long as possible and keep the score close. Next day, more than a tad nervous, we began play and had a really good game with the Saskatchewan girls. Though we lost, we were really proud of how well we had played against this magnificent team.

At the Closing Ceremonies, the top three teams were presented with gold, silver, and bronze medals. We climbed up on the podium and received the medals just like in the Olympics. The next day on the flight back to Ontario, we all wore our medals around our necks for fun as did the athletes from other sports. About an hour or so into the flight, I was talking with one of my teammates and we were looking at our inscribed medals when I had my moment of epiphany. It was as if I had been hit by a bolt of lightning. I looked down at my silver medal and thought, "I wonder what would have happened if I had played the game to win?"

It was a moment of complete awareness and clarity – I realized, too late, that we had conceded the victory to our opponents in our minds, that we had allowed ourselves to be so impressed with what they had achieved that we had decided to "settle" for second, to play to make it look good, to affirm for all and ourselves that we were the next best team because we were the only ones to give them a tight game.

I cannot tell you how vivid that moment is in my mind – it was 34 years ago and it was yesterday. Suddenly, the silver medal I had been relishing a few moments earlier looked like a pretty poor consolation prize. To this day it irks the heck out of me – not that I lost, but *how I chose* to lose, because I will never know if we could have won if we had had more confidence and really tried. I realized that the true joy in sport is the challenge for excellence and I had unconsciously retreated from the challenge. And I resolved that never again would I sell myself short. This crystal-clear moment on a plane high in the sky somewhere over Saskatchewan or Manitoba truly became the defining moment of my life.

Since then, I have not always finished first or won the things for which I have aspired. But from that moment to this day, I have never retreated from a challenge that appealed to me. While I fully accept the limitations of my God-given skills never again have I allowed myself to be confined by self-imposed limitations of will.

I still have that little silver medal. It has become golden to me. I look back on what I have done, where I have gone, whom I have met, and I know, without reservation, that the moment of awakening on that plane 34 years ago has defined my adult life.

In the end, sport is not about what you achieve, it is about who you become.

PAT REID competed in three Canadian Women's Curling Championships, is a member of the Canadian Olympic Association (COA) Board of Directors, and was Team Leader for Curling in the Olympic Winter Games in Nagano, 1998. She was the recipient of the Bryce Taylor Memorial Award for Volunteer Leadership.

GAETAN BOUCHER

In the summer of 1983 I trained hard to overcome a serious ankle injury. As soon as I started skating again in October 1983, I knew the efforts would pay off. I was skating fast and had no trouble defeating all my opponents many times in the weeks prior to the Olympics. I was confident I could not be beaten. I proved it in Sarajevo at the Olympic Games in 1984 with two golds and a bronze. My main competitor there was a Russian by the name of Chlebnikov. He had finished second to me twice.

Two weeks after the Games, we were in Norway for the World Sprint Championship, which is a combination of four races: 500 metres and 1,000 metres the first day and 500 metres and 1,000 metres the second day. Points are awarded based on a 500-metre time. Forty seconds for a 500-metre race means 40 points. The 1,000-metre time is converted to seconds and divided by two. The winner is the skater with the lowest point total.

I had not lost a 1,000-metre race in over a year. At the Olympics I had won by almost one second, an impressive margin in a sport often won by hundredths of seconds.

On the first day of competition, Chlebnikov and I skated the 500 metres within 3/100 of each other. Then I skated my first 1,000 metres with a decent time that I didn't think anybody could beat. I went to my dressing room and was riding the bike when one of my teammates came in and said, "Chlebnikov beat you in the 1000 metres."

"You're joking!" I could scarcely believe it.

"No, I'm not. And not by a little. He beat you by almost half a second!"

I did not think much of it, finished my ride, and went outside for the medal ceremony. Each day there is a medal ceremony even though the overall champion is not crowned until both days are completed. On the podium, as Chlebnikov received his gold medal, he looked at me and said, "Revenge, Sarajevo."

That night back in my room, before going to bed, I was signing autographs on a pile of pictures – almost 500 of them – brought to me from Canada. Speed skating in Norway is an important sport and being Olympic champion made me very popular among the younger kids. I had been asked to sign the pictures so I could give them away once the championship was finished. Then an idea struck me. Instead of just signing my name on the remaining 50 unsigned pictures, I now wrote: "Gaetan Boucher, World Sprint Champion 1984." I had not even won the championship yet, and making up half a second with two races to go would not be easy. However, I believed I could do it.

On the second day of the championship, Chlebnikov and I again were within a few hundredths of seconds of each other in the 500 metres. It was now up to the last 1,000 metres to decide who would be the world champion. I calculated that, in order to win, I would have to beat Chlebnikov by 47/100. The good thing was that I was paired with him and I knew he tended to tense a little too much everytime we skated against each other.

My strategy in the race worked perfectly. Chlebnikov never relaxed and rushed his movements instead of skating his own race. I won the race by . . . 49/100 and became world champion.

Chlebnikov and I met later on the podium. He went home with a silver medal . . . and a signed photograph from the new world champion!

GAETAN BOUCHER is a speed skater who was a double gold medallist and bronze medallist at the Olympic Winter Games in Sarajevo, 1984, and a silver medallist at the Olympic Winter Games in Lake Placid, 1980. He also represented Canada at the Olympic Winter Games in Innsbruck, 1976, and in Calgary, 1988. He was the first Canadian speed skater to win a gold medal at the Olympic Winter Games.

CLAIRE CARVER-DIAS

Twelve years ago I chose to don a pair of noseplugs and give synchronized swimming a try. I was horrible. My clumsy 11-year-old body couldn't seem to master the right moves to the right timing with the music. At my first National Championships I sat on the side and watched as my team swam to a marvellous sixth-place, pink-ribbon finish.

At the end of my first and second years, I placed a new "Participation" trophy on my shelf . . . but I swam on. I had developed a strange adoration for the sport I had adopted and a determination to just "be good."

There was no real turning point in my journey. It never came easy. I just worked hard and pursued a dream of being "good." But mostly, I just never gave up. Recently I added an Olympic bronze medal to my collection of Consolation and Participation trophies!

CLAIRE CARVER-DIAS was on the Canadian Synchronized Swimming Team that won a bronze medal at the Olympic Games in Sydney, 2000. She has also won two World Cup bronze medals.

• 10 •

GET BACK ON THE HORSE

Before high school I considered myself to be quite a formid-
able competitor. Really, I was just a big fish in a small pond.
My first year of high school was the Atlantic Ocean compared
to the bathtub I'd been swimming in! At our area champi-
onships, this hit home when I did so poorly that I didn't even
qualify to go to the qualifier for the qualifier for the provincial
high school championships! I knew that I loved to run and I
had now learned exactly how much I disliked losing. The
next day I joined the Burlington Track Club.

– Graham Hood, member of Canada's Track and Field Team,
Olympic Games, Barcelona, 1992, Atlanta, 1996

PATRICK JARVIS

On a sunny July day on the Prairies in 1967, a simple slip on a stool in the local butcher shop set me on a whole new life path. As summer casual help, I wasn't even supposed to be working on any equipment but I was, and as one could expect with a child – I was eight – working around machinery, there was an accident and I was at the centre of it. There were going to be a lot of adjustments after my accident, some of the biggest concerning how I'd continue with my passion for sports. In a small rural community, sports is the social lifeblood and already at my young age, sports was an important part of my life. Losing my left hand in a meat grinder meant there were going to be some significant changes – or would there be?

The first day I was fully recovered from the anaesthetic, the gruff old English surgeon who had performed the operation walked into my hospital room and placed a take-away box from the local fast-food joint on my table. He made quite a performance of removing the contents – fries, a chocolate shake, and a hamburger. "Time to get back on the horse, lad" was all he said as he handed me the hamburger. The episode threw me at first, but the grin, twinkling eyes, and demeanour with which he delivered the simple line spoke volumes about getting on with things. It was my first lesson in the power of action. He really was delivering the lesson about not worrying what had happened but focusing on what to do now. The burger was a good metaphor but the test of truly getting "back on the horse" would happen once I was back in the routine of life.

A couple of weeks after I came home from the hospital, our family was visiting a favourite aunt in the town of Bashaw. I loved going to visit as the days were always filled with the joy and laughter of close family and friends. My aunt's was a very modest place, a tiny home with two bedrooms precariously attached at the rear of the house, almost as an afterthought. What it lacked in size it made up in character; it was the type of place that nourishes wonderful moments that become fabulous childhood memories. This was my first visit as an amputee, and I can only imagine the trepidation and anxiety of my parents and relatives as to how I'd adjust.

Characteristically, my two older brothers were the ones to expedite an answer to the unasked questions. In a family of six children, there was never a shortage of siblings to find a way to occupy lazy Saturday afternoons, whether at home or away visiting. At my brothers' behest, we headed out to the gravel road that ran in front of the house. They wanted to throw around the football, as we often did, simply tossing it back and forth, pretending to be famous players from our favourite CFL teams. It dawned on me as we went out the front door that this was to be my first real test, my first real sport experience since the accident. Inside, I was silently praying that the horse I was about to get back on would be gentle.

My brothers were encouraging, supportive, and perhaps wise beyond their years. Michael, my oldest brother, had me stand very close to him and coached me once again on the fundamentals of catching a ball. "Remember, see it into your hands . . . well, you know, your hand and your arm . . . and then cradle it gently into the body. It's simple, keep your eyes on the ball." To illustrate the simplicity of the task, Michael had David throw him the football a couple of times. Then it was my turn. It seemed all so familiar but my anxiety was mounting.

To me, sport has always been much more than simply winning. At first it was all about just playing, enjoying the activity at a base, visceral level. As I matured, I came to recognize that in many ways it was a microcosm of life, teaching its participants about character and deceit, accomplishment and adversity, and helping them discover a fascinating spectrum of emotions. The moment I was about to face, on an empty street in front of my aunt's house, was about the most important aspect of sport, self-esteem. I was about to do battle with myself and all the self-perceptions that would emanate from this simple yet profound act of playing catch.

The ball seemed to be hurtling at me from outer space, yet Michael was all of ten yards away from me when he threw it. I closely followed its trajectory, remembering to move my feet to get into the proper position and then steeled myself for the actual catch. All of a sudden doubt seemed to fade away, indeed the world seemed to disappear, as my entire being was now focused on catching this football that was descending from the bright afternoon sky. I reached out with my right hand and instinctively my left hand followed, although all that remained was a short stump below the elbow. Time slowed as the leather first contacted my fingers and I pulled the football in toward my body, my left arm wrapping in behind it to ensure that I didn't let the ball fall to the gravel below, followed closely by my hopes and self-worth. The ball came to rest and I had it safe and sound in my arms. A feeling of relief and joy overcame me, and no doubt those feelings were even more intense in my brothers' hearts. I confidently tossed the ball back to my brother, my grin pushing back against my ears. This wasn't hard, nothing else should be either. And that was it, I was back on the horse.

PATRICK JARVIS was a member of Canada's Paralympic Team in Barcelona, 1992, running in the 800 and 1,500 metres. He was Chef de Mission at the Paralympic Winter Games in Nagano, 1998, and is currently president of the Canadian Paralympic Committee.

CARRIE FLEMMER

The year I was in Grade 11 my older sister brought me home an Olympic pin when she went to Los Angeles during the 1984 Olympic Games. I wore that pin everywhere and decided my goal was to collect pins from all the future Olympics. A week went by and I wasn't sure if I was going to be satisfied just collecting the pins, so I thought I would attend the Olympics as a spectator. A couple more weeks went by and I asked myself, "Am I going to be satisfied just collecting pins?" No. "Am I going to be satisfied by going and watching the Olympics?" No. That is the day I realized I wanted to be *in* the Olympics!

I did not know exactly what sport would take me to the Olympics (I enjoyed many) so I kept involved in everything, but softball was definitely my favourite. Eventually I was invited to a training camp for the National Softball Team. Once a year, a week-long selection camp is held and from the 30 invited to the camp, 15 to 19 are chosen to be members of the National Softball Team.

I was invited to my first selection camp in 1985. I was excited but terribly nervous and it was a frightening experience for me. Everyone goes home on Saturday, and on Sunday morning, the coach calls to let you know whether you made the team. When the coach called, I wasn't surprised I hadn't made it. He said he knew I could perform much better so maybe I'd be invited back next year.

The next year I was invited again. This time the week was great. I performed much better, I wasn't as nervous, and I knew what to expect. When I got home, I waited for my call Sunday morning. When the coach called, he explained that I was much better than last year but . . . he still did not think I was good enough for the team.

The third year I had a fantastic camp. I did well the whole week. Sunday found me waiting anxiously by the phone. Coach called and once again said how well I played but . . . he still did not think I was good enough for the team. Very disappointed, I asked him why not. He thought I was not big enough and I needed to gain weight (just what every girl wants to hear!). As a catcher, I needed to be much bigger and stronger. I immediately went on a training program and started lifting weights.

The fourth year I was much stronger and it was my best camp ever. Sunday I got the call. Coach told me he was thrilled at how much stronger I was but . . . he still did not think I was good enough. Frustration and depression were setting in but again I asked how I could get better. He told me I needed to be faster. Another training program – weights and sprint training.

The fifth year – you've heard it before – I had my best camp ever. I was faster and stronger. Saturday night I was nervous and Sunday I got the call. The coach said he could not believe my improvements but . . . he still did not think I was good enough. Sad, sad, very sad. How could he do this to me? I'd done everything he asked me to do. This time he said I needed more experience. That was perfect timing because I had just received a full softball scholarship in Louisiana. I would be playing tons of games, so experience – here I come.

The sixth year, with loads of experience, strength, and speed, I was back at camp in full force! This was it, this was my year! After a week of physical and mental exhaustion, I went home knowing this was the year. By now, most of my friends had made it in their fourth or fifth year, and those who had not made it quit or simply were not asked back.

The call came and I was so excited. The coach quietly told me he was very impressed with my experience and abilities but . . . he was choosing not to take me . . . again. I was angry and let him know that his decision was outrageous. It was so wrong. How could he do this to me? I slammed the phone down.

I felt as if I was a complete failure. I didn't want anything to do with softball ever again. I went to the garage, threw my glove in the garbage, and grabbed my tennis racquet and some balls. I went to the grounds of my elementary school and hit the ball against the wall hard. I played tennis for hours. After I had time to cool off (one year later), amazingly the Softball National Team coach called me to go back for the seventh year.

Biting my lip, I agreed to go back. What did I have to lose (other than my sanity)? I really did love the sport and I totally enjoyed playing it. Once again, I had a tremendous camp. I was hitting home runs, throwing people out at second base, and leading the team with real confidence (everyone knew me by this point, I'd been around for so long). Sunday I got my call. Coach thanked me for returning to the camp and then said, "Congratulations, Carrie, you've made the team."

I was so excited, I didn't know what to do or say. It had taken me seven painful years, years when I thought I was a failure but years that were stepping stones to my goal of being a National Team member.

I remained on the team for six years, until 1996, my final year – when, at the age of 28, I finally played in the Olympics!

CARRIE FLEMMER competed as a member of Canada's Women's Softball Team at the Olympic Games in Atlanta, 1996. She was the catcher for the Canadian Women's National Team for six years.

JEFF TIESSEN

In 1977 my life took a 180-degree turn. I went from being a regular kid with regular talents, regular interests, regular relationships, and regular kids' dreams and ambitions to a special kid who was often told things like "You probably won't be able to do this or that." I became more comfortable with doctors, nurses, therapists than I was with kids my own age. And my ambitions went from playing second base for the Detroit Tigers to learning how to use a fork and knife someday.

But this isn't a sob story. Actually, it was the foundation for what I consider a success story. If that 180-degree turn hadn't happened, I'm sure I wouldn't be a world record holder, and I wouldn't have travelled to far-off places. I had to become my own best advocate. I had to learn that the words "You won't be able to do that" could become a source of inspiration. And I had to resist the temptation of the comfort zone that people were offering me and my disability.

My goals were to learn to do everyday things all over again – dressing, riding a bike – and learning to do those things were big accomplishments and sometimes were hard to swallow. It was hard for an 11-year-old kid to get too excited about learning to open a door or comb his hair.

As a regular kid, I'd been expected to cut the grass, shovel the sidewalk, be nice to people, but after my injury that changed. I didn't like this change in attitude and expectations so I felt it was up to me to do something about it. Those experiences forced me to continuously reset my goals, although very small goals. I was becoming more independent, more confident, and more determined to be treated like everyone else. Soon it became a habit to set goals that were slightly out of my reach.

One of the greatest decisions that my parents, being great advocates for me, made on my behalf was something I opposed with all my might. Looking back, it might have been the single most important decision they made for me. I had always been a pretty good athlete but they had instilled in us that it was more important to give your best or do the best with what you're given than it was to be the best.

My dad enforced this soon after I was out of the hospital when I was just starting to learn how to use my artificial arms. I had played hockey before my injury in Leamington's minor hockey league. My dad's attitude was "You can still skate – you can play hockey again." I argued that not having two hands was the problem, not the skating part. Night after night, he worked in his shed, rigging up a stick that would work for my artificial hands – holes in the shafts, mechanical attachments on the end. Then one Saturday morning it was time. With tears of fear streaming down my cheeks, we left for the arena. I'm still not sure who was more courageous that day, me or my dad. So much was at stake for the both of us. Today, as an adult and dad myself, I see how dramatically my life was shaped by my father's determined effort to see me included in my community hockey league. Without a doubt, it was the most influential decision my father ever made for me. Because I came to know that "if I could play hockey again, I could do anything."

JEFF TIESSEN, a runner, won a gold medal at the Paralympic Games in Seoul, 1988, and a bronze medal at the Paralympic Games in Barcelona, 1992.

SHARON DONNELLY

It happened in an instant: the screeching and rending of metal, rubber, and plastic; the cries of anguished competitors;

the world tumbling insanely; and the pain of hitting the asphalt, other competitors, and their bicycles. My Olympic dream of winning a medal at the first-ever Olympic triathlon disappeared in mere seconds in a major crash during the bike portion of the women's event. Essentially, it was a lifetime of work and dedication to competition wiped out. But I have come to terms with my Olympic race and I have never been more proud of myself.

On competition day, I had walked to the race area and could feel my stomach doing somersaults – I was here – the Olympics! The atmosphere was electric and the number of spectators already lining the route two hours before the start was huge. I saw my family in the stands and I waved and smiled at them, though they were probably more nervous than me.

I had not drawn a good start position for the swimming event; it was on the far side of the diving pontoon. I spent the majority of the time fighting to get to the centre, where the better swimmers were, and my coughing seemed always to coincide with a big wave pounding into me. But I didn't panic and left the water about 30 seconds behind the first pack of women – there are usually 6 to 15 women in a pack. I knew if my pack worked together, we could catch the front pack. But we didn't get that chance.

I was travelling over 40 kilometres an hour when the two girls directly in front of me touched wheels and went down. I braked so hard that I put a hole through my tire. I had no room to manoeuvre around them so I knew I was going down! I piled into the barrier and then onto the pavement. I bounced right back up, but I had broken the rear wheel on the barrier. All I could think of was getting back into the race.

I started to run with my bike to the next wheel stop. The course is six loops of 6.6 kilometres each and there are six places to change wheels on the course. Also, if the front group of competitors laps you, you are pulled off the course and can't finish. A race official offered to take my wheel and go to the other side where the wheel change was. I waited an eternity for a spare. Meanwhile, as other competitors raced by, the girl who crashed in front of me was still crying and moaning in pain (she had broken her collarbone), a Japanese competitor in a daze with blood on her face struggled to get her bike back in order, and nearby spectators tried to comfort us. I kept saying, "I gotta finish, I must finish . . ." I also thought of my friends and all of Canada watching TV at home and I just couldn't quit.

As each minute passed, I was getting more concerned that I would not get the chance to cross the finish line, something I had worked so long and hard to do. Finally after about six minutes, the mechanic ran up with spare wheels and got me on my way.

It then became a time trial with the front group and myself. "Don't let them catch me" was all I could think. I was bloodied and my back and elbow were hurting quite badly but I didn't notice. The front group wasn't far back, but I managed to hold them off for the duration of the bike race. It was very tough to come into the transition area, to start the run, alone in last position. The crowd was huge and the cheers of my family and other Canadians rang loud and clear through the other cheers for me. I was in tears. The run was so tough, more mentally than physically. My body was in rough shape, my neck was killing me, and for 10 kilometres, thoughts of my ruined Olympic dreams rushed through my mind. There are no words to describe what I was going through. But I knew that at least I could finish. Of the other 11 women who had crashed, only two of us were able to finish. I crossed the line in 38th position out of the 40 competitors who completed the race. I was in tears, but I also had a smile on my face – I had come to terms with myself during the race and I had to finish with my head up and be proud.

The morning following my race, I received so many e-mails I could hardly read them all! Those e-mails are what really helped to get me back on my feet and allow me to enjoy the remainder of the Games – the outpouring of kind words from friends, from children I had never met, from parents all saying that they were proud of my performance and courage and that I was a great role model for children. I nearly short-circuited my computer from all the tears falling on the keyboard!

I finally had achieved my goal of competing in the Olympic Games. Of the many quotes I had stuck on my wall that summer for inspiration, little did I know that this one would be the one to define my Olympic race: "Our greatest glory consists *not* in never falling, but in *rising* each time we fall."

SHARON DONNELLY competed in the Triathlon as a member of the Canadian Olympic Team in Sydney, 2000. She won a gold medal in the Triathlon at the Pan American Games in Winnipeg, 1999.

• 11 •

UNEXPECTED HEROES

My dad was important to my continued success in basket-ball. He would drive four hours on the weekend to come and see me play. And then he would turn around and drive four hours home, no matter the weather, all by himself.

– Norman Clarke, member of Canada's Basketball Team, Olympic Games, Seoul, 1988

FRANCE ST-LOUIS

In 1998 I was a member of the Women's National Hockey Team, which was spending six months in Calgary training for the Winter Olympics in Nagano. It was sometimes very hard on us physically and mentally being away from family and friends and training six days a week two times a day. I was the oldest on the team at 39 years of age, and trying to make the Olympic Team was the biggest challenge of my hockey career. There wasn't anything more important to me.

One day during that long process I was sitting in the dressing room, a little depressed. I was tired. Nothing was going well on the ice and I was afraid I would not make the team because of my age. As I was sitting there, I saw a card addressed to me and on it were these words:

> In every journey, there is meaning.
> In every conflict, there is growth.
> In every action, there is purpose.
> In every moment of doubt, remember to BELIEVE in yourself . . .

That card was from the youngest player on the team, Hayley Wickenheiser, 19 years old. Coming from her it had special meaning and had a huge influence on me right away. It helped me to refocus and keep going and most of all "believe in myself" no matter what, no matter how old I was.

FRANCE ST-LOUIS was on Canada's National Women's Hockey Team that won the silver medal at the Olympic Winter Games in Nagano, 1998. Her team won gold medals in five World Championships, 1990, 1992, 1994, 1997, and 1999. She was captain of Team Canada from 1992 to 1994.

NADINE ROLLAND

I was trying to qualify for the Olympic Team for Sydney in the 50-metre freestyle swim. It was August 3, 2000. Only the top two would go – and I missed the second spot by 1/100 of a second! Jenna Gresdal and Marianne Limpert had tied for first. I was in tears, devastated. Two hours later my coach, Patrick Clement, told me that Marianne Limpert had decided to give up her spot in the 50 metres in order to allow me to go! She would compete in other events in Sydney and wanted me to have the opportunity as well. I was ecstatic and so touched by her generous gesture. In Sydney I missed the semifinals by only 8/100 of a second but at a World Cup meet in Washington two months later, I became the fastest Canadian girl ever in the 50-metre short course. Marianne's selfless act provided me with the opportunity of a lifetime, one I will never forget!

NADINE ROLLAND was a member of Canada's Swim Team at the Olympic Games in Sydney, 2000. She is a 17-time medallist on the World Cup circuit, 2000–2001.

ALDO ROY

The weight on the bar was 170 kilograms. That's what my coach and I thought I needed to lift for my third and final attempt in the clean and jerk in order to make the Canadian Weightlifting Team for the 1968 Olympics. The battle took place on the afternoon of August 3 in the hot, spacious gymnasium of the University of Calgary. My best ever in this lift was 162.5 kilograms and I had just accomplished that moments before. If I made this lift, it would not only be a Canadian Senior record, but would secure my chances of making, for the first time, Canada's Olympic Team.

Everything I had dreamt of was wrapped up in this lift. Instead of getting caught up by the past and the moment, I tried to focus on the finer points of the lift. The first stage of the lift was going to be easy, but I also was aware that a torn ligament in my left elbow was going to show its ugly head in the second stage, the jerk.

Sure enough, the clean was like a feather. Suddenly this monstrous weight was on my shoulders and I was bouncing out of the deep squat position in order to set up for the second part of the lift. I drove the weight to arm's length and assumed the classic deep split position, but no sooner had it hit the slot than it began its unceremonious and disrespectful journey downward and abruptly crashed to the platform! My ambition to wear Canada's Olympic uniform crashed with it. In 1960, I had just missed making the team and in 1964 a severe injury had left me out of the running again. Now at the age of 26, I was not going to be on Canada's Olympic Team ever!

In any weight division, the maximum number of competitors allowed was two per country. In my weight division, 82.5 kilograms, three of us had qualified but only two could go. Pierre St.-Jean, Canada's premiere lifter of the sixties, had finished first. On his tail was Paul Bjarnason of Vancouver. And I was third. My disappointment was clear for all to see during the medal presentation. Tears flowed freely and few words were exchanged.

That evening, Paul approached me. He was simple and direct. "Aldo, how would you like to go to the Olympic Games?" Right away I knew what he was offering. Paul had already assured himself a spot on the Olympic Team by qualifying in another division, the 90-kilogram weight category. He explained that he had entered in my weight category to compete against and beat Pierre St. Jean. Nonetheless, I also knew this was an act of unselfishness, unparalleled in the annals of Canadian weightlifting history.

That night, throughout the celebrations, I could not stop thinking of Paul's kind gesture. Because of him I was and would always be an Olympian!

Paul's decision proved to be a tremendous sacrifice. At the Olympics, he caught a bug and had trouble maintaining his bodyweight above 85 kilograms. His results were nothing to write home about, but in light of what he had sacrificed for me, his performance was truly Olympian. As I helped him pack his gear, I wanted to thank him and tell him how much

I had appreciated his selfless act. But perhaps due to my age or the fact that in those days men did not talk about feelings, I let it ride.

Thirty-two years later in June 2000, through the marvel of the Internet, I opened an e-mail from an unfamiliar name. To my surprise it was Paul Bjarnason. I had not been in touch with him for over 30 years. I wrote back immediately, finally able to write the words I had not been able to say. I thanked him for his Olympic sacrifice and asked him to tell the story to his kids because it showed something so incredibly special about their father. I said, "I truly hope that your 1968 Olympic experience is enhanced by what you did for me. Such acts are more important than the actual competition."

Shortly after, I received his reply:

"No, I've never forgotten the 1968 Olympic trials in Calgary – what a meet that was! – I have a vivid image in my mind of your effortless 374 clean, just like a toy! As for my sacrifice, I think you may be giving me too much credit (I know you would have done the same for me), but nonetheless your words mean very much to me. I never really knew just how you felt, but I'm glad to read the heartfelt expression of your feelings on the situation. . . . You and I both know just how difficult it is to 'merely' qualify for an Olympic Team. I've always felt that in 1968 we both deserved to go, and I'll always be glad that we both did go. In truth my 'sacrifice' was not much compared to the injustice that would have come your way by a selfish refusal on my part to lift in another weight class. . . . In the years since I've never wished to go back on that decision. And now that I know your feelings on the matter, I feel it as a welcome confirmation of all that has gone before. But remember, the only thing I did was to agree to lift in the next weight class; you fully earned your place on the Olympic Team by meeting the Olympic Standard, no less difficult then than now, all things considered.

"You are quite right when you say that there are more important things than the actual competition. Friendship and mutual respect are far more meaningful than lifting a certain weight or winning a particular contest. And I can tell you truly that my memories of the 1968 Olympic experience are very much enhanced by my having read your letter as well as by my having done what was right at the time."

When people try to reach for the stars, sometimes good and unexpected things occur. What remains are the memories and good deeds of all those around us, those who in one way or another help us attain the impossible.

ALDO ROY was a weightlifter and a member of Canada's Olympic Team in Mexico City, 1968. In 1980, he was a coach for the Canadian Olympic Team.

FRANK CANNARELLA

We were at the 1996 Ontario Games, the pre-qualifying competition for the 1996 Paralympic Games in Atlanta. The hotel room in which my friend and I were staying was above the pool deck, and when we opened the curtains, we could see the pool below. It was a day or two before the competitions were to start, and I was on the balcony, looking out over the pool getting mentally prepared for the upcoming events. My friend, Jimmy Primavera, came out to join me, and as we began talking about how nervous we were and how we were going to get focused for our competitions, one boy down below caught our attention. He was a young disabled athlete, no more than 14 years old, and we stared at him as he made his way across the deck to the edge of the pool. I stood there half in shock, half in anxiety, anticipating this boy's next move. The question I had was "How is he going to swim with no arms or legs?"

As Jimmy and I watched silently, the boy took a deep breath and to our amazement dove into the water and started swimming with the little amount of strength that was generated from his short limbs and stumps. His action floored both of us, for as we looked at this eager young boy we realized that we didn't have it as bad as we thought. I am a paraplegic and my friend is a quadriplegic and we thought that life had its challenges, but after witnessing this kid we felt blessed.

That weekend the competitions were held, and thanks to the inspiration of that scene in the pool, I won silver medals at three different events. At the end of the weekend, at the traditional banquet to celebrate the events that had taken place, once again this boy caught my attention and awed me. During one of the dances after dinner, I saw him jump enthusiastically out of his chair, race onto the floor, and start dancing with a young girl. I was almost in tears for this boy had taught me in the simplest possible way, without even knowing it, the value of perseverance and optimism. All I could think was that there was nothing that could stop this kid. I realized something that I have carried with me since. No matter what we have in life, injury or otherwise, we all have the capability to do something and overcome obstacles that stand in our way. There's no reason we all can't go for our dreams. I never did approach the boy during the competition or after, but if I had I would have thanked him whole-heartedly for giving me the courage and desire to continue to overcome the challenges that stood in my path.

FRANK CANNARELLA has participated in sports as varied as wheelchair racing, rowing, power lifting, discus, shot put, and javelin. He is a member of the Canadian National Wheelchair Fencing Team and has been ranked number one for Épée and Foil fencing in Canada.

LORENE HATELT

I first went to the Triathlon World Championships when they were held in Ohio in 1998. The day of the race I met a fellow competitor, Bob Wieland. Bob was much older and had the biggest arms I had ever seen. He was a competitor in the wheelchair division and was one of the most intriguing people I had ever met. After losing his legs in Vietnam, he went on to become the strength coach for an NFL football team. He had completed a marathon, not in his wheelchair but by walking *on his hands! He later walked across the United States on his hands!*

I will never forget meeting the man with the big arms, a true hero. It taught me a lesson that day. I always *thought* that just about anything was possible, but now I *knew* it was!

LORENE HATELT was the World Triathlon Champion in Les Autres division, in 1998, 1999, and 2000.

· 12 ·

OH NO!

As I went to accept my prize – third in the second group in skeet shooting – the presenter tried every variation of my name. Handing me my award, he said, "I sure hope you don't shoot this game more often so I don't have to pronounce your name." My embarrassment turned to determination and I vowed silently, "You'd better get used to pronouncing it, spelling it, and knowing it as well as you know your own because I intend to be on this podium again!"

– Don Kwasnycia, skeet shooter, member of Canada's Olympic Team, Moscow, 1980 (boycotted Games), and Seoul, 1988

SYLVIE BERNIER

When I was 16 or 17 years old, I was the top Canadian in diving and was in the top 10 in the world. I used to chew a lot of gum to control my stress level. I mean a lot of gum – one piece was never enough. I would put many, many pieces into my mouth and chew and chew.

I was attending a competition in Mexico. We would take a bus to the event site, and on this particular morning, I was sitting at the very front of the bus, with all the divers, judges, and coaches farther back. As usual I was chewing a huge wad of gum. When I'd finished chewing, I took the gum and threw it out my window. All of a sudden I heard everyone on the bus laughing hysterically. I looked back and couldn't believe my eyes! My gum was stuck to the cheek of the judge at the very back of the bus! It had gone out my window and was blown back into his window right onto his face! Everyone knew it was me who did it, because of my reputation for chewing gum. I have never been so embarrassed in my life. A half hour later, there I was in the competition performing for the very same judge. His cheek was bare and he had a twinkle in his eye but I swore then that my gum-chewing days were over!

SYLVIE BERNIER won a gold medal in the three-metre Springboard Diving competition at the Olympic Games in Los Angeles, 1984, and was a silver medallist at the Commonwealth Games in Brisbane, Australia, 1982.

JAMES RANSOM

Perhaps the most significant experience I have come across in my 12 years in the sport of fencing happened, appropriately, at the highest point in my career. At the Olympic Games in Atlanta, amidst newspaper headlines expounding on the transportation nightmares, our team had decided to request a private shuttle bus to take us to the venue earlier than the scheduled ACOG (Atlanta Committee for the Olympic Games) bus. The plan was simple: On the morning of the competition a volunteer shuttle arranged by ACOG was to pick us up at the gas station immediately outside the gates to take my two teammates, my coach, and me to the venue with time to spare.

After we had spent a leisurely hour and a half at our new digs at the gas station, the terrified and extremely apologetic volunteer for ACOG arrived; before we had time to complain about the delay, we were speeding along the highway. Another hour passed as we dominated the passing lane and rapidly made up for lost time. Naturally, this lost time would later have to be added to our account, plus interest, when we arrived at the gates of the wrong venue, conveniently located on the opposite side of town from our own.

The terrified volunteer had now cracked. She sobbed uncontrollably as she drove, huge volunteer tears dribbling out from under her volunteer sunglasses and falling on to her Olympic pin-studded collar. I tried to tell her that everything would be all right but she was beyond consolation. My subsequent remark about how I thought we could make it to our venue on time prompted our coach to interject, "Maybe you should start warming up now, James." Another huge sob came from the volunteer, who had managed to shrink to nearly half her original size and was dividing her time between crawling down the seat to use the pedals and peeking over the dashboard.

Our arrival was a blur of running and shouting, which strangely subsided when our coach checked the schedule of matches and determined that among us it was only I who was doomed by our sightseeing tour that morning. I remember something about a fencing competition some five to seven minutes later, and then my first and only Olympic bout was over.

JAMES RANSOM was a member of Canada's Fencing Team at the Olympic Games in Atlanta, 1996. He was Canadian champion in 1996 and 1997.

MAXINE ARMSTRONG

I walked outside the clubhouse, and froze mid-step. I was in 18 inches of water. All the fences and light standards were down, and the bleachers looked like a new art form. I don't know if it was my state of shock or if there really wasn't any air to breathe. With one hand on my heart and the other over my mouth, I couldn't believe I had experienced my first typhoon.

I had wanted a tryout for the Women's National Softball Team, and the only way to improve my skills was to play in the off-season somewhere else. Australia answered my call. In the fall of 1983 I left Toronto to go to the other side of the world, where I didn't know anyone.

When I got to Hong Kong, I was told there was no room on the flight to Melbourne. The next flight wouldn't be until Thursday. This was Tuesday. I asked at the airport for assistance in finding accommodation. There was good news – there was a room – and bad news – the room was $350 U.S. a night. Oh, and by the way, Ms. Armstrong, we can't locate your luggage. I sat down on the little bench beside the counter and started to laugh, thinking about my friends who were envious of my adventure.

A young airline employee, Kan, told me I was lucky to get the hotel room and should take it – Hong Kong was notorious for room shortages. Kan and I spent the next day taking in the sights and promised to stay in touch.

Thursday morning, I checked out of the hotel and headed to the airport. It was wild outside. Ferocious winds and raging rain were bombing Hong Kong. I watched people nailing boards over windows. What was going on? At the airport I discovered that all flights were cancelled. A number 8 typhoon was scheduled to hit the mainland this evening. Now I was beginning to feel abandoned and scared. What was I going to do? I headed back to the hotel and learned that they could not accommodate me. The magnificent Meridian hotel lobby was packed with families and their luggage, with nowhere to go. The only thing I could think of was to call the Hong Kong Softball Association.

"Hi, my name is Maxine Armstrong. I am a Canadian soft-ball player stuck here in Hong Kong, en route to Melbourne, Australia, and I was wondering. . . ."

"Why didn't you call me when you arrived?" was the response. Oh my god – he spoke English and he knew me! I was speaking with Ross Sinclair, a Canadian teacher from Thunder Bay who had relocated to coach the Hong Kong Women's Softball Team. He told me to stay put, he was on his way to meet me. It was easy to identify Ross when he entered the hotel lobby. He was about 6 feet 2 inches with carrot red hair. "Let's get out in it!" he said. I asked, "Out in what?" He replied, "The typhoon!"

We made our way to the softball clubhouse where there were a number of Hong Kong's national softball team players just hanging out. I think they were intimidated by my different looks and my size, not to mention the communica-tion challenges. I was just happy to have a place to stay. The clubhouse was an old aluminum barn-shaped building, with a restaurant in the front half and an office with an old couch in the back half. I curled up on the couch, eventually fell asleep, and the next morning when I woke up . . . well, that's the scene at the start of my story!

Even with the typhoon over, my travel plans were still a problem but the airline was able to put me in the jump seat, the little seat that pulls out of the wall right behind the pilot. I was to leave Saturday night.

From afternoon on Friday to early Saturday evening, I was on the ball field. The players were like sponges. They wanted me to teach them everything I knew. Pitching, batting stance, bunting. Although we couldn't understand each other well, we communicated through sport. They made me promise that I would stop on my return trip so we could continue our play. And I did. I have stayed in touch with everyone I met during those few days.

Committing to something caused me to step out into the world and completely throw myself off balance. In the process, I could feel myself grow as a person and an athlete, and I wouldn't change a single element!

MAXINE ARMSTRONG was a member of the Canadian Softball Team in the Olympic Games in Los Angeles, 1984, and a member of four Canadian Championship Softball Teams.

STEPHEN CLARKE

Olympic trials! Easily the most stressful competition any athlete will ever experience, the trials are a one-shot chance an athlete gets every four years. Everyone is on edge at this meet, the swimmers, coaches, parents, and officials. My first experience at Olympic trials was in 1992 in Montreal. It was incredibly exciting; the thing that struck me was how hundredths of a second could decide whether an athlete was ecstatic or devastated! Although I had qualified for Canada's Olympic Team by winning the men's 100-metre freestyle, my story is not about that race — it is about the 50-metre freestyle on the last day of trials. It was the most bizarre race I have ever been involved in.

The 50-metre freestyle is the shortest race in swimming. It is one lap of the pool — as fast as you can go. Not much strategy is involved. But it is highly stressful because it has to be perfect – a bad start, bad breakout, or bad touch and the race is lost. This race is on the last day of trials, so the stress level increases as you get closer to it. It is the last chance for many athletes to make the Olympic Team – losing could mean waiting another four years or even retiring.

The prelims are held in the morning with seven to 10 heats and the fastest eight swimmers from the preliminary heats swim in the final that evening. Only the top two in the final will go to the Olympics, providing they make the qualifying standard.

The start is critical. Every swimmer tries to anticipate the start, tries to judge the starter's rhythm. You sit behind the block and listen to the early heats and study the starters. (Do they hold the start? Are they fast?) This event usually has the most false starts, and this morning there were a tremendous number of false starts. With every false start the crowd grew more anxious and the swimmers became more agitated. The crowd and swimmers were getting increasingly angry with the starter (even though it was not her fault), but as the abuse grew and the false starts increased, there was pressure to get the heats done. In the end, I got through the heats as the number five seed – all you need is a lane in the final.

During the afternoon several swimmers who had not made the final protested that their start was unfair, that not all swimmers were set before the start. The officials reviewed the evidence and decided that two of the heats needed to be swum again. Because the swimmers were back at their hotel, it was decided that those two heats would be swum at the start of the finals.

Eight swimmers had been preparing all day for the finals, but when they arrived at the pool, they learned there were two heats to be re-swum. If any of the swimmers in those two heats were to beat the time of any of the current final eight, those current finalists would be out. After the re-swim, three swimmers were bumped. Now there was trouble!

The bumped swimmers complained that *they* were in the final, and the three new swimmers said *they* were in. When the men's 50 free was ready to be marshalled, 11 guys showed up for the final – in a pool that had only eight lanes! We sat there for 45 minutes while the officials and coaches argued over what to do. The best thing would have been to just re-swim the next day, but this was the last day of the meet. The crowd was getting restless and the officials told us to just march out for the final. As we walked down to the pool (all 11 of us), people were confused and laughing. We did not know what to do when we got behind our lanes. The meet was stopped for another 10 minutes and finally they decided to run two finals – a final of the three new guys and then the final of eight. With everyone so keyed up, there was not a clean start in the second final. The winner missed the Olympic standard by a few hundredths of a second. The meet ended with protests and meetings, and while we went out for a night to celebrate and to drown our sorrows, the officials tried to sort things out.

The next day we were told that the decision about the 50-metre swim final was that it would be re-swum the following day, in two groups if necessary, at another pool across town. Ironically, there were now only eight of us swimming. Three swimmers had already flown home!

The scene at the pool was unusual. Here we were, showing up for finals at Olympic trials. The stands were empty. In the pool about 40 kids ranging from eight to 12 years old were having a practice swim. The eight of us stood around stretching and thinking how weird this was. The Canadian Broadcasting Corporation had sent one camera to film this bizarre scene. The kids were told to move over into four lanes so we could use the other four to warm up. It was very strange to be warming up with the other seven swimmers. It was so hard to get the excitement and focus back. The official came over to tell us it was time. As I stood behind the block, I could not help but laugh. On one side of the pool were 40 wet, cold kids looking very upset that they had had to clear the pool so we could race. On the other side of the pool were eight coaches with stopwatches and one CBC cameraman. In the stands – well, the stands were still empty.

The one thing that this story is missing is a happy ending. Predictably, no one made the qualifying standard and therefore no Canadian would go to the Olympics to compete in this event. I was almost one second off my best time. I felt badly for some of the swimmers who had had a good chance of making the team. They had not had a chance to perform under circumstances that would allow them to show what they could do. Although I was already guaranteed a trip to Barcelona, the other swimmers had been cheated of a chance to compete at these Olympics.

STEPHEN CLARKE was a bronze medallist in Swimming at the Olympic Games in Barcelona, 1992, and a member of the Canadian Olympic Team in Atlanta, 1996. He was a gold medallist in Swimming at the Commonwealth Games, Victoria, 1994.

NANCY OLMSTED

As a naive 18-year-old girl from Northern Ontario, I had no idea what was in store for me as I embarked on my first ever Olympic Games in Los Angeles, 1984. I had just graduated from Grade 12 at Widdifield Secondary School in North Bay and had spent the winter months training in Florida with the veterans of the women's canoe and kayak team, eight to 10 years my senior. I knew only too well that qualifying for the 1984 Olympics was a long shot, but nonetheless it could be a growing experience that would develop my career.

To my surprise, I did qualify for the Olympics and was the youngest member of the Canadian Canoe/Kayak Team. The rest of the dream is all quite a blur, but the most memorable and most anxiety-provoking experience involved my teammates and their own version of the rookie initiation. Every female who participates in the Olympics is required to endure a sex test, Princess Anne being the only exception. At the time, I was unaware of the particulars of this test. To say the least, my naïveté got the best of me. The girls on the team had me scared out of my wits, telling me that the doctor would have to do a full pelvic exam and a strip search to determine that I was a legitimate female! In an attempt to scare me even further, they even spoke to the attending doctor before my exam. I was thoroughly convinced that a full examination was required. Much to my relief, the doctor smiled at me and told me what the girls had asked of him and comforted me when he explained that all he needed to do was scrape cheek cells from my mouth!

By the way, I passed the test!

NANCY OLMSTED was a member of Canada's Canoe/
Kayak Team at the Olympic Games in Los Angeles, 1984, and
Seoul, 1988. She has won over 50 national championship
medals.

· 13 ·

TOUGH CHOICES

My father died six weeks before the Olympic trials. Among everything drifting inside my mind and in my heart during the next weeks was whether I should still compete in the synchronized swimming trials for the Olympics. Although I had lost the competitive fire, I decided to finish what I had started. I returned to my team. Pain, anger, sadness, frustration, self-pity were tangled in a distraught mind and exhausted body. I had many sleepless nights; my goggles hid many tears. Throughout all this I trained — when I wanted to, when I didn't, when it felt good and when it didn't. I did it because my dad had fought so hard to see us for those last few days and that gave me no right to give up when I was so close to going to the Olympics. He had been a fighter till the end, and I constantly drew strength from that.

— Jessica Chase, Olympic bronze medallist, Canada's Synchronized Swimming Team, Olympic Games, Sydney, 2000

PAUL HENDERSON

The experience associated with the Olympics which has remained with me most vividly was reinforced when my wife, Mary, and I were in Sydney for the Olympic Games in 2000. We were invited to the Jewish School to commemorate the anniversary of "Black Tuesday 1972," the day Israeli athletes had been murdered in the Munich Olympics.

In 1972 the sailing venue was in Kiel, Germany, 500 miles north of Munich. I was coach of the Canadian Team, and early the day after the massacre, I got a phone call from the Chef de Mission in Munich saying that at the request of the IOC, I had to poll the Canadian Sailing Team about what they wanted to do.

There were three options:

1. Cancel the Games.
2. Cancel all events involving Israeli athletes.
3. Have two days of mourning.

I had no idea what to do, and the atmosphere throughout the venue was very depressing. I looked out the window of my room and saw, sitting on a bench, alone, one of the best

Canadian sailors and now a famous Toronto lawyer, Allan Liebel. It immediately hit me that since Allan was Jewish, he was the only one who could properly give an insight into what should be done.

I went down and sat beside Allan and told him the options. He immediately replied, "We should be racing today, and the Games must immediately go on. If we stop, the terrorists, whose only raison d'être is to disrupt normal human behaviour, *win!*"

I have always governed my life by that day.

PAUL HENDERSON was a member of the Canadian Sailing Team at the Olympic Games in Tokyo, 1964, Mexico City, 1968, and Munich, 1972. He is the president of the International Sailing Federation and a member of the International Olympic Committee.

MARNIE McBEAN

Three weeks before the 2000 Sydney Olympics, my third Games, I went for my first row at our final training camp. It had started much like any other practice but after 10 minutes I was completely overwhelmed by indescribable pain. I had rowed two kilometres from the dock and was unable to return. My coach had to come by in his motorboat to get me. Together, we were able to get me from my boat onto the floor of his, where I lay in pain as he drove us back to shore. I had noticed before this that a hamstring was tight but was unaware of any pending back injuries. The team physiotherapist instantly diagnosed a herniated disc, but I was in denial. That evening we saw a doctor, and he too right away diagnosed the same thing. I was outnumbered. Within three days I had the results of an MRI in my hand that was indisputable. It was just as the doctor said – there was "bad news and really bad news." My pain was definitely the result of two herniated discs, one of which had ruptured, and the really bad news was it wasn't going to be better in time for the Games. What else could I do but cry?

For the next five days, I kept the results of the MRI to myself. I told no one, not my coach, not my teammates; I had to absorb this news first. My season had not been going well but I had been sure I was on the verge of shaking whatever mystery had been slowing me down. My technique was solid, my training aggressive (but also appropriate and well thought out). Something had been missing and now the doctors were telling me it was this link in my back that had been sabotaging my power.

What were my options? Go home, wallow in self-pity and disappointment? Cry and whine in front of my teammates, dragging down the mood and excitement of what was still their final Olympic preparation? Stay and watch, put myself right in front of a dream that I have so long believed was mine to make come true? Watch a teammate row in *my* boat, in *my* event, at *my* Games? How would I be able to do that and show a stiff upper lip? I had no idea how but I knew I had to stay.

Kristen Wall, a young rower who had gone to Australia as an alternate for the eight, was designated to be my replacement. Through the year Kristen and I had become close friends, each supporting the other when we were away at training camps. She had come to my house in Toronto for

Thanksgiving when we were at training camp in London, Ontario, and I had gone to her family house when we were training in Victoria. I think had it been anyone else I would not have handled it so well, but for Kristen, I got excited. At the last minute her family made arrangements to come to Sydney and watch their daughter race. Tickets were hard to come by and I was able to arrange to get them tickets that my aunt and uncle had purchased. I contacted the boat builder and arranged that the personal name tagging that is on each Hudson-manufactured boat be changed from "Marnie McBean" to "Kristen Wall" – I wanted to be sure she felt she had some ownership of the event. I showed up early for her races to hang out with her in her pre-race prep.

I watched all the races. I even went to the Opening and Closing Ceremonies. I lived in the village for a week and went to a variety of events – water polo, synchronized swimming, diving, swimming (kind of a water theme!). Through all this, I was getting extensive treatment from team physiotherapists, massage therapists, and chiropractors. I was on two different types of pain medication (both were still legal for competition!) but I couldn't sit at all without pain shooting down my leg. When I wanted to cheer, I would have to bend my knees to release the strain on my nervous system. When I travelled, I lay down on bus and van benches and a few times I was even lying on the floor in the back cargo space of a minivan.

I was physically a mess. But staying in Australia and opening myself up to let in the experiences and excitement of the other rowers and other members of the Canadian Team was one of the most rewarding things I have ever done at an Olympics.

MARNIE McBEAN, with former rowing partner Kathleen
Heddle, is Canada's most successful Olympic athlete – she
holds 12 World and Olympic medals, three of which are
Olympic gold, two from Barcelona, 1992, and one from
Atlanta, 1996. She is the only rower to have won a medal in
each of her sport's disciplines.

MOOREA LONGSTAFF

May 26, 1996: Today is the day I've been looking forward
to for the last 365 days, the last 52 weeks; the day that
has been in my dreams, in my thoughts. Today is the first thing
I think of when I wake up in the morning and the last thing I
think of when I go to bed at night.

As my palms begin to sweat, I feel my heart beat faster
with every breath. I know there is no looking back. A million
and one thoughts race through my mind. I know that in the
next 10 minutes, my life will change forever. There is nothing
that I can do but sit and wait. With every second that goes by,
it feels like an eternity.

Five minutes. Four. Three. Two. One. I count the seconds.
As I stare at the official, he starts naming the top 13 swimmers
who have qualified for the Paralympic Games in Atlanta,
Georgia, that summer. I have been thinking of all the thousands of hours of gruelling work that I've put in to get to
this moment.

Number 1, number 2, number 3, number 4, number 5,
number 6, number 7, number 8, number 9, number 10,
number 11, number 12, number 13 . . . then number 14

Moorea Longstaff – first alternate! My heart begins to race, I feel like there's been a mistake, it can't be true. My eyes begin to water. I stand for a moment in complete and utter shock.

I know then exactly what I have to do.

As I walk toward my teammates, an enormous smile appears on my face. I spend the next 60 minutes congratulating the new Canadian Team. As I watch the 13 best swimmers in Canada get their uniforms, I remember something I once read in a book: "Failure is the compost that grows success."

I wrote these thoughts five years ago when I was 13. That was the worst day of my life.

It was also the best day of my life because I knew my time would come and when it did, it would mean more to me than it would have on May 26, 1996.

MOOREA LONGSTAFF is a swimmer and was a bronze medallist at the Paralympic Games in Sydney, 2000.

DAN THOMPSON

Dateline: April 22, 1980

Westbound on the 401 express lanes between Avenue Road and Yonge Street. "Good afternoon, it's 3 p.m. and time for the CKFM afternoon news Tuesday, April 22 and our top story of the day, Mark MacGuigan, minister for external affairs, today announced Canada's participation in the 1980 Olympic boycott. Canada today joins the 14-nation boycott of the Olympic Games to protest the Soviet Union's invasion of Afghanistan." The announcer drones on but by now I'm deep in thought.

We all knew this day was coming and, frankly, it came as no great surprise – but it was quite surreal to actually hear the news driving to the Etobicoke Olympium to continue my Olympic training. At 24, I had put my degree on hold to pursue my Olympic goal.

Somehow I had come to grips with the whole notion of the boycott. Yes, it was pointless and, yes, we all knew Canada would be selling wheat to the Russians within six months.

The Olympics is supposed to be about peace and understanding – it just didn't make any sense. I daydreamed about going – and then I realized that it wasn't remotely possible. I thought, I'll quit and play golf, my first sport, but I knew I'd kick myself down the road. I couldn't control the situation and I did feel cheated, because I knew that in 20 years making the Olympic Team and being a role model for the sport community would have some importance.

I arrived at the Olympium, feeling the warm air as I entered the pool, smelling the chlorine, and hearing the high-pitched buzz of the lights as they warmed up. Word spread fast, and Deryk Snelling, our coach, had prepared us pretty well for this day. I remember the pep talk in the storage room off the main pool. In among the lane line reels and the starting blocks we gathered. Deryk, in his red shirt and white shorts, put a brave face on the situation but he lived for the Olympics and his disappointment was obvious. He encouraged us to keep going, to keep this moment in perspective, and make the team. There were a few tears and a few choice words aimed at the American and Canadian establishments, but we all knew the boycott was real and that none of us would feel the emotional rush of walking into Lenin Stadium for the Opening Ceremonies.

We swam as we always did that day but the mood was reserved, very little was said, and everyone was deep in thought. I guess it had all been said for us.

Sport is just one component of one's life and not an all-encompassing philosophy of life itself. My Olympic experience was a great lesson in perspective.

DAN THOMPSON, a swimmer, qualified for Canada's 1980 Olympic Team but declined to participate in alternative competitions that summer. He was ranked fourth in the world in 1979 for the 100-metre butterfly.

• 14 •

LET THE GAMES BEGIN

I remember the thrill of walking into the Opening Ceremonies and making the trip around the track before 80,000 people. What could be better than someone calling out your name: "Pauline, Pauline!"? It was my dad. I'll never forget the look on his face as we exchanged waves. My heart took a picture of that moment and I'll cherish it always.

– Pauline Maurice, member of Canada's Softball Team, Olympic Games, Atlanta, 1996

JODY HOLDEN

There is nothing like going to an Olympic Games as an athlete. The anxiety and anticipation levels are so elevated that even the veteran athletes have trouble nodding off on the flights to the Games. There's such a strong sense of not wanting to miss one moment of the experience that everyone's mind is unusually sharp. Then, you finally arrive at the Games and everyone has gone to extravagant lengths to make you feel at home and take care of you.

You are quickly ushered through administrative check-ins, given your athlete's identification card, and shuttled off to the athletes' village. The moment you walk through the police-controlled, secured gates of the village, you feel as if they have opened the floodgates to happiness. Just imagine being surrounded by 13,000 athletes, coaches, and volunteers and each and every one of them in the same euphoric mood that you are in! You can feel the electricity in the air because it really is that strong.

JODY HOLDEN, with his partner Conrad Leineman, won a bronze medal at the Beach Volleyball World Championship

Tour stop in Brazil, 1997, and was a member of the Canadian Olympic Team at the Olympic Games in Sydney, 2000. They also won gold at the Pan American Games, 1999, the only time Canada has won gold in this sport.

MARGO MALOWNEY

O pening Day at the 1996 Atlanta Olympic Games. We have been herded from our rooms to meet outside our residence. We're on our way to the Opening Ceremonies. We're dressed in our Canada stuff: round, white, wide-brimmed hats with a ribbon; calf-length, light rose-coloured linen and silk skirts; long-sleeved, round-collared, white button-up blouse, dark rose-coloured vest; burgundy one-and-a-half-inch-heeled ankle boots and a matching purse. (The guys are dressed slightly differently.)

Outside, we take pictures of each other before we head to the buses. We follow our team leaders alongside the residence buildings and onto the sidewalk. Running along one side of the walk is a stone wall and trees, whose boughs and branches overhang the sidewalk. The other side is lined by rows of buses, running and ready to depart. The beautiful overhang of branches serves to capture the heat and exhaust fumes of the buses, and we are a little overwhelmed. Atlanta is stifling hot. We try our best not to sweat in the heat and humidity, which only makes us sweat more. We board the buses and are off.

The buses drop us off at the "small" stadium beside the newly built stadium where the ceremonies are to take place. We are directed to a stand where we can pick up frozen lemonade and Olympic lunch boxes containing snacks to sustain us during the wait ahead. The plan is to keep the thousands of international athletes in the small stadium, to watch the festivities, the parades, and speeches on the JumboTron, then march us in. After the arrival of the athletes there's only the arrival of the flame and the official opening of the Games. We are warned that we might be on the field for up to four hours . . . and to take note of the absence of any Porta-Potty. Our challenge is to determine just the right balance between dehydration and possible extreme discomfort later.

In the small stadium we are seated alphabetically by country. The ceremonies begin next door and we watch them on the Jumbotron. Soon everyone is trying to figure out the best way to stay cool. The skirts quickly become miniskirts; the guys are trying not to get too close to their own shirts . . . we wait and we sweat. Our hats make great fans. The show seems to be spectacular on the big screen. We wait, we sweat. We wait some more. We see fireworks from the other stadium over top of our own. It is time.

Anticipation builds, although most of us have no idea what to expect. As the athletes are led out of the small stadium to the big one, the anticipation is palpable. The nervousness and excitement are tangible.

We wait. We sweat. Being from Canada we assumed we would be close to the beginning of the roll call. Technically that is true, but in fact, Canada is the 35th country out of 137 in alphabetical order. Canada. C-A-N . . . 35th. Thirty-fifth! On the Jumbotron in front of us we can see the athletes ahead of us filing out of the small stadium. The empty seats move closer and closer to where we are seated. Finally it is our turn. We have been waiting forever. We move toward the exits.

Suddenly there is a cry. . . . "There is a huge gap – you'll have to run!" Run? We've been waiting forever and now we're late? Somehow, in all that waiting, there has been a delay in the march. We sprint out of the small stadium, across the tarmac, and up a metallic ramp leading to the other stadium. Security personnel are calling "Hurry . . . run!" We run up the ramp, to be confronted with what seems to be an impenetrable wall of mist and lights and the deep rumbling roar of the crowd. We have entered the stadium. At the top of the ramp, we look out at thousands of people through a heavy, damp, humid fog, illuminated by flash bulbs and spotlights. It is the most overwhelming sight I've ever seen. Shell-shocked, we stand there for what seems an eternity, then our senses return and we realize we have been sprinting. We tuck our blouses back into our skirts (the guys tuck their shirts into their pants), straighten our vests, put our hats on, and begin the march into the stadium.

All I can hear is a thunderous cheer when Canada enters. There are Canadians everywhere we look. Flags of all sizes waving all around. Cameras everywhere. People smiling, yelling, laughing, and waving. All I can do is wave back. And wave. And wave. As many times as I've done a lap of a track in my life, none will ever parallel this one.

As suddenly as it starts, it ends. Our lap is over. Already? I'm sure it has taken me longer to round a track in high school. We line up to await the entry of the rest of the athletes in the 1996 Olympiad.

The rest of the ceremonies are a blur. Individually, we "travel" a little and visit with friends from Australia and Brazil while the other 100 countries take their places. As quickly as it passes, it also seems to take forever.

The final country to enter the stadium at any Olympic Opening Ceremonies is the host country. As the Games are in the United States, naturally they are the final leg. They typically have an enormous contingent because they have the population to support it.

The Dream Team (II) enters as a separate country somehow – they do not march with their fellow American athletes. Céline sings. The flame arrives and is handed to Muhammad Ali. With a shaky hand (one of the most emotional moments of all) he sets the torch alight. The 1996 Olympic Games are declared open.

MARGO MALOWNEY was a member of the Canadian Beach Volleyball Team at the Olympic Games in Atlanta, 1996. She was the bronze medallist at the World Championships in Los Angeles, 1997.

GEORGE GROSS JR.

It was the day of the Opening Ceremonies for the 1983 Pan Am Games in Venezuela. The Canadian contingent had been told to be dressed and downstairs in the athletes' village by 12:30. It was about 1:15 when we got back from our water polo practice that morning so we were already late, and six of us were to be in the Opening Ceremonies. Three immediately ran to get changed. I'd been to a few events in my time and I knew athletes were told to be ready two hours before they really needed to be so I said to the other two, "Let's go and have lunch." We finished eating by 2:00 and as we left the lunch hall, the buses for the Canadian contingent were leaving the village for the 35-minute drive to the city where the Opening Ceremonies were being held. My two friends were now upset that they were going to miss the ceremonies, but I said, "Don't worry, there are more than 75 countries so we'll hop on the last bus with the Venezuelans since they're the host country and will be going in at the end. We'll get off the bus and find the Canadian contingent and march with them." They agreed.

We headed back to the rooms to change but I suggested we have a nap first! Forty-five minutes later we got up. I went to the window and saw there were still 26 buses – "We've got lots of time," I said. When I looked out again, I could see the Venezuelans gathered, waiting for their bus, so we headed downstairs.

By the time we got downstairs, though, the village was empty. There were still 26 buses sitting there, but no people! We ran around trying to find out what had happened. It seems the army had ordered the extra buses . . . just in case. We tried to get on one, but the soldiers wouldn't let us, and even though the buses were empty, they pulled out, driving exactly to where we wanted to go!

The ceremonies were due to start at four o'clock and it was now 3:35. At the front gate we saw a van with three or four people in it who were going to the city to shop. I asked the driver, "When are you leaving?" He said, "In about 15 minutes." "Not good enough," I said, "we've got to leave now." "Can't do it," he said. I pulled out a Canadian Olympic pin and he said, "Okay, we're going!"

It normally took 10 minutes to get to the highway – this time it took three. He drove on the sidewalk, on the fields, across the road, and we made it to the highway quickly and in one piece. I figured we could do it – we would make it there by 4:15 and Canada, being the 12th country to go in, would not march into the stadium until 4:25. Meanwhile the driver was still going fast. Then it began to drizzle a bit and the van started to glide. We had no speed. "What's wrong?" I asked.

"No gas!"

At the bottom of the hill there was a truck stop with gas pumps; meanwhile it was raining harder. We glided into the gas station, pulled up to the pump, and stopped. The driver called to the attendants to come and give us gas. No way – they weren't coming out in the rain.

I approached the fellow who was supposed to be pumping the gas and said, "We've got to get some gas."

"Can't do, raining."

I pulled out another pin.

"Oh, sure! Lots of gas!"

Once we got the gas in the tank, we took off. Now it was ten to four and we were about 20 minutes from the stadium. When we finally made it to the university, the Venezuelan athletes were just getting off their buses.

"Hey guys, we're okay, no problem," I said to my two friends.

We made our way through the Venezuelan athletes and were looking for the Canadians but couldn't find them. Just as we got to the top of the ramp that led to the stadium, we saw the last row of Canadian men going up the track as part of the Opening Ceremonies.

We had to make a decision. We could run down the ramp, across the ramp, and catch up to the last row, in which case 70,000 people, the entire Canadian contingent, the entire

world watching on TV, and worst of all my mother would see
three of us running along the track trying to catch up to our
team! So I said, "No, we can't do that. My mum will have a
heart attack." After thinking a bit, I said, "Listen guys, we'll
jump in with another country, we'll walk around a bit, then
slip out into the Canadian section when they're lined up on
the field."

Then who came by but Cuba! Six hundred athletes, red
and white country. No problem! The three of us jumped into
line, right beside the water polo team and we started walking
down the ramp with them. When we got to the bottom of
the ramp, an organizing committee official saw us in the
middle. He didn't want us with the Cubans so he pulled us
out of the line. Now we were at the bottom of the ramp and
we could see the Canadians, separated from us by eight
lengths of track, 20 lengths of turf, and four rows of soldiers!
We didn't know what we were going to do.

We were right by the entrance where the athletes came in.
The athletes would march along one side of the stadium, then
the far end, then into the middle of the field. So there was a
whole side with about 8,000 fans who didn't get to see the
athletes close up. While we were standing there, a fellow came
up and said, "¿Qué pasa?" – What are you doing here? I said,
in a mixture of English and Spanish, "We're 15 minutes late
and missed coming in with our country. They're over there."
He suggested we all go up in the stands and watch from there,
but I said, "No, no, we want to be with our country." Then,
in perfect English, he said, "Follow me." We started walking
with him, right in front of the fans who were farthest away
from the spectacle. They hadn't had anyone go by them, and
they weren't going to, so when they saw three athletes walking

by, they started to applaud! I said to my buddies, "You guys got pins?" They did. "Let's wave," I said. So we started waving to the fans and they started applauding louder. I said, "Grab your pins!" We each took a handful of pins from our pockets and heaved them into the stands. Eight thousand people gave us a standing ovation. We ran through the soldiers before they knew what was happening and joined the Canadian contingent.

The three of us got a bigger ovation than 75 of 77 countries there!

GEORGE GROSS JR. was a member of the Canadian Water Polo Team at the Olympic Games in Montreal, 1976, and in Los Angeles, 1984. He was a two-time bronze medallist at the Pan American Games.

SUE HOLLOWAY

I have participated in events in places as small as Burns Lake and as large as Los Angeles. I have been to small local events and I have been to the greatest sports event in the world.

The first one that stands out in my mind is the Canada Games I attended in Saskatoon. There aren't a lot of hills in Saskatchewan to hold the alpine events so they built a hill – out of garbage! Those Games were a favourite for another reason – the people. Everyone you met was so friendly and excited about having you in their town. I was only a teenager but kids would run up to us all the time to get our autograph. Not only did the organizers have to deal with a lack of hills, there was also a lack of accommodation. The athletes' village was a vacant downtown department store! The main floor was filled with little trailers where you usually see the jewellery and accessories; other floors had cots and tents that might have been borrowed from the army. I'm not sure if I would be quite so keen to live like that today but when I was 15 it was great!

Nothing, however, comes close to preparing you for the biggest event of them all, the Olympic Games. It is wild, especially if you come from low-profile sports – cross-country skiing and kayaking – like me. The sheer magnitude of the Games throws you, especially the Summer Games. The Winter Games seem like an elite country club. I might be having lunch in the cafeteria with Ken Read or Toller Cranston! And over there is Vladislav Tretiak and over there is Ingemar Stenmark. I almost fell down the stairs when I walked by Franz Klammer.

The Summer Games by comparison are just sheer numbers. It is like a circus. The hardest thing to adjust to is the village itself. For starters there is a 24-hour cafeteria. Some people have been known to eat themselves out of competition! The movie theatres show all the latest movies, there are concerts with major stars, the latest video games, virtual reality games, shopping, hairdressers, massage – and it's all free! Here you are, supposed to be resting, and there's all this great stuff to do!

But nothing can match the Opening Ceremonies. I have had the good fortune to walk in two of them, both in 1976. The first was in the Olympic Winter Games in Innsbruck, where I competed in cross-country skiing. We looked as if we had escaped from the Russian Imperial Army, wearing long dark blue wool coats with capes lined in red satin and lovely white knit hats, which the boys were very happy to wear (not!). Roots Canada provided the boots and they were those negative heel things that were popular at the time. When we were standing on an uphill slope, waiting to go into the stadium, our calf muscles got so stretched we all turned around and stood backwards. All the other countries were in a row and Canada was standing facing the wrong way.

There is a lot of hurry up and wait to the Opening Ceremonies, but it is all worth it when you hear the announcer say "Canada" and you step into the stadium. I was marching beside another first-timer, and as we walked in we reached out to each other at the same time and squeezed hands. Even though it was cold outside, I had a wonderful warm feeling inside and a grin that wouldn't stop.

My next Olympic Games was the Summer Olympic Games that year, and it was a different experience. The team is three times bigger and we were competing at home, in Montreal. All the countries were marshalled in the Olympic Village for the short walk over to the Olympic Stadium. Olympic athletes are fairly independent individuals, a characteristic that has worked well for them in sport. However, it does not work well when you want them to march together in straight lines! A military fellow was assigned the impossible task of getting us lined up and staying lined up. It was not going well. Just when it seemed things were starting to come together, the Snow Birds air show flew by and everyone scattered to watch them. It was fortunate that the host country marches in last because we needed the extra time to get back in some semblance of order. As we made our way around the track, the outpouring of emotions was overwhelming. It was as if everyone across the country was sending us their energy and support. The Olympic Spirit wrapped itself in my soul that day. I still feel it when I see our flag, when I watch the current generation of Olympians perform, and when I follow my kids out on the ski trails.

SUE HOLLOWAY was a member of Canada's Cross-Country Ski Team at the Olympic Winter Games in Innsbruck, 1976, and a member of Canada's Canoe/Kayak Team at the Olympic Games in Montreal, 1976, Moscow, 1980 (boycotted Games), and Los Angeles, 1984.

SIMON WHITFIELD

My goal had always been to get to the Olympic Games as a medal contender. So on September 12, 2000, when I arrived in the athletes' village in Sydney, Australia, I felt I had accomplished my goal. I believed that the winner of the Olympic triathlon would be whoever could put all the preparation together and was relaxed and confident. But ultimately it would come down to who wanted it the most.

Not only was I a contender for a medal, I knew I was going to have an incredible race. Three days before my race, on Thursday, I went running at 7 a.m., jogging around the village for 10 minutes and soaking in the atmosphere. The village had its own grass track, which must have had 100 people from around the world training on it. I ran my first one-minute interval, felt pretty good, and tried to think back on all the training I had done. I did the next two-minute rep and was starting to get into my rhythm. On the three-minute interval I felt like I was floating and had to hold everything back not to run a world record on the Olympic Village grass track.

Finally, on the last two-minute interval, I couldn't contain it – I felt unbelievable. Everything was flowing. When the interval was done, I just stopped, stood there, and was absolutely confident that this was it. It was all right. I jumped up and down, with a feeling I can't describe. Everything had come together and I was standing at the side of a track, at the Olympic Games. I knew, at that moment of pure excitement, that great things happen to people who make great things happen and I was about to put on one heck of a show.

SIMON WHITFIELD was the gold medallist in Triathlon at the Olympic Games in Sydney, 2000. He was a bronze medallist at the Pan American Games in Winnipeg, 1999, and was Canadian Triathlon champion in 1998 and 1999.

· 15 ·

WE ARE FAMILY

It was the World Cup, Mexico, 1986. Our soccer team was standing in the tunnel next to the French team waiting to come onto the field. I remember looking down the line of all those famous players, captained by the great Michel Platini, and thinking how before I had only been able to watch them on TV, and now here I was about to play them in the World Cup! Though we were foes on the playing field, we were brothers in the great sport of soccer.

– Bob Lenarduzzi, member of Canada's Soccer Team, Olympic Games, Los Angeles, 1984; member of Canada's World Cup Team, Mexico, 1986

LINDA CUTHBERT

I think my most enduring memories are those from outside competition. I remember sitting on the side of the pool deck with the Russian divers and exchanging tongue twisters. They were a lot better at doing our English tongue twisters than we were at doing the Russian ones! I also remember a train trip to a competition in Bulgaria. We were singing songs with the athletes from Mexico and Cuba. This was one of the many times I experienced both music and sport as the universal languages that bridge cultures and peoples.

And then there was the time in China in 1980. Canada had boycotted the Moscow Olympics so the Canadian diving team went on a demonstration tour in China. China was just beginning to open its doors to the Western world, and our Chinese hosts were quite hospitable. One day, while on a sightseeing tour with the Chinese divers, we walked up a hill and stopped at a pagoda-like structure for a rest and a cup of tea. It was somehow indicated to us to go ahead and entertain ourselves. Entertain ourselves. No video games, no TV, no radio, not even a deck of cards. Imagine. The Chinese divers led the way by singing a song and we were expected to reciprocate. This went on for a while, singing songs back and forth. Then the Chinese divers told us through their interpreter that they knew one song in English and would be happy if we would sing it with them. So there we were on a hot August day sitting in a pagoda in China singing "Jingle Bells"!

LINDA CUTHBERT won a gold medal at the Commonwealth Games, Edmonton, 1978, and bronze medals at the Pan American Games, Mexico City, 1975 and San Juan, Puerto Rico, 1979. She was a member of the National Diving Team from 1972 to 1980 and was Canadian champion four times.

ADRIANNE DUNNETT

Music plays a big role in my two most poignant memories from competitions.

I was at a gymnastics competition in a huge arena in Bulgaria, in 1983. My teammate and I had finished our round, so we were sitting in the stands with some Bulgarian friends, watching the second half of the competition. This was at a time when the Iron Curtain was still firmly in place, so when all the lights suddenly went out in the middle of a routine, we felt somewhat anxious about what was happening.

The audience was completely silent. As our eyes adjusted to the dimness, we saw a figure move across the floor of the arena. Then through the dark came piano music. Beautiful music – classical, jazz, pop.

For an hour, the capacity crowd didn't budge as we listened to the pianist for the Portuguese team. When the lights finally came on, he simply jumped up and trotted back across the arena floor and out of sight. He didn't acknowledge or even seem to hear the thunderous applause. It was the best concert I've ever been to.

My second memory concerns my very first international competition. I was using a piece of music that had been composed by the pianist for the West German team. He was a quiet old man, with a craggy, empathetic face. And through the years of my competitive career, we came across each other in gymnasiums and arenas all over the world. We never spoke a word to each other, but whenever he was sitting at the piano and would see me with my team, he would play a few bars of that music and give me a conspiratorial smile.

It's been years since I've seen Philipesco's face, but I feel connected to him, even today.

ADRIANNE DUNNETT represented Canada in Rhythmic Gymnastics at the Olympic Games in Los Angeles, 1984. She was a member of Canada's Rhythmic Gymnastics Team from 1977 to 1984 and competed in four World Championships.

ROBERT FINLAY

I have often been asked what it was like to be at the 1972 Munich Olympics. How did it feel to be an athlete in the Olympic Village when the dreadful massacre of members of the Israeli team took place? That these young men, who proudly represented their country as top sportsmen and coaches in their fields, were used as pawns in a game of

terrorism was bad enough. That their lives were cut off so
violently was the cruel price they and their families paid for
the honour of representing their country in sport.

At the time, the athletes in the village knew far less about
what was going on than did our families and the rest of the
world. As the events played out, watched by world media,
we were aware of a serious crisis involving Arabs and Israelis.
But we did not have the informed reporting of the press, nor
the exact details of the demands of the terrorists.

The tragedy will forever be part of Olympic history. On
the morning of September 5, 1972, two Israeli coaches were
shot and killed when Arab commandos broke into the Israeli
residence in the Olympic Village. Nine other members of the
team were taken hostage. As the world watched and waited,
negotiations took place between the West German officials,
the Israeli government, and the Arab commandos. Their
demands for the release of political prisoners were rejected.
With two Israelis dead already, the world was stunned, but
no one expected the disastrous outcome for the remaining
hostages. After hours of negotiations, arrangements were
agreed upon and late that evening the captors and hostages
were transported from the village, first by bus and then by
helicopter, to a military airport. Hindsight is, of course, wonderful, and whether the situation was mismanaged or not will
always be open to debate. A shootout took place at the
airport, and the remaining nine hostages were killed, some by
gunfire, and some by grenades thrown into the helicopters
where they were still sitting, tied up.

When I woke up on the morning of that dreadful day, the
events were just starting to unfold. One of my roommates
told me that the Palestinians had taken a number of the Israeli

athletes hostage. I was still half-asleep and thought it was a far-fetched story and didn't believe it. I soon learned the truth. From the balcony of the apartment building we were staying in we could see through the building next to ours and into the one next to it, which housed the Israeli team. We could faintly see masked men holding what we assumed to be semi-automatic guns.

For me, immersed in my own concerns of performance, the biggest disruption was that my race was delayed by one day. I, like other competitors, had to readjust final training plans. Understandably, security was tightened dramatically. On that morning we were told to leave our residence, taking everything we would need for that day, including training equipment. We had to sneak out of the residence and edge along the fence behind our building. Normally we would have taken a path that went by the Israeli residence onto the main path leading through the centre of the village. As the day wore on, the security was lax at times and then tighter at other times. Some of the other athletes were able to get back to our residence (by sneaking along the fence, the same way we had left that morning). I never did get back to the village until late that evening and the only news was generally in German so I did not really understand what was going on.

The next day a memorial service was held, which most of the athletes attended and the Olympic events for that day were cancelled – or at least postponed. I don't think the severity of the whole disaster sank in immediately, as I was too engrossed in my own training and how I was going to do in my race. Those of us in the village still did not have the whole story. When I did realize the magnitude of the event, which was probably only after I had left the Games, I felt the pain of it all.

At that time I felt violated, as if this was an action taken against all Olympic athletes. I could not understand why an organization had to use such tactics to get its point across and waste the lives and abilities of so many young athletes. Again politics was playing a bigger part in the Games than the events themselves and what they were originally set up to portray. What a bitter ending to these Olympics where the flame burned as always to symbolize purity, the endeavour for perfection, the struggle for victory, as well as "peace and friendship."

I have often wondered if I lined up for food behind one of the murdered athletes the day before it happened. Did we pass in a hallway, united by a passion for a particular sport, having trained for months and months to exhaustion, scarcely daring to dream of competing at this level? They were strong and fit, just like me, with an agenda like mine. The excitement, the thrill of being there at the Olympics, was probably foremost on their minds. As a team they wanted to achieve, to perform well, to make their countries and families proud. They had walked in the Opening Ceremonies, fully expecting to participate in the Closing of the Games two weeks later. This was the fun stuff. Had they lived they would be in their 50s now, like me, with grown children and even grandchildren.

ROBERT FINLAY was a member of Canada's Track and Field Team at the Olympic Games in Mexico City, 1968 (to date, the last Canadian to have made it to the finals of the 5,000 metres) and Munich, 1972.

VICTORIA WINTER

In 1995 I had the opportunity to represent Canada in my first major senior international competition, the Pan American Games in Argentina. Along with my horse Wedgwood ("Woody"), I was a member of the Canadian Dressage team.

In order to prepare our horses for the summertime conditions they would encounter in March in Argentina, the four team members and two alternates spent a three-week acclimatization period in Florida. The horses made the 36-hour trip in a large commercial van complete with video monitors to allow the drivers to keep an eye on them at all times.

Woody arrived safely in Florida, although a little tired and very confused at the weather change! His winter coat had already been clipped before leaving Canada; however, he still suffered from the heat. He also broke out in hives as his body got used to the different bugs Florida had to offer.

Due to agricultural restrictions we knew we would not be able to take our horses' regular feed with us to Argentina. We were given a nutritional breakdown of the feed that would be available at the Games and tried to find similar feed in Florida. We gradually started to introduce this feed to our horses so they would be more accepting of the Argentinian food. This was of particular concern to me as Woody is a very picky eater.

The morning of our departure day arrived and we loaded up and headed to the Miami airport. By that time, my coach, Neil Ishoy, and our team vet, Alan Young, had arrived to travel with the horses. One thing I have learned over the years is that travelling with horses is never without complications.

When we arrived at the airport we were told that the flight
was delayed, so we took the horses off the trailer and put them
in concrete stalls at the airport. With all the noise and com-
motion at the airport, Woody was very nervous and kept
running around the stall refusing to eat or drink. I spent hours
scratching his favourite spot at the bottom of his neck trying
to get him to settle. The delay stretched through the day, and
soon we found ourselves trying to get some sleep on the concrete floor next to the horses (while keeping an eye out for
the mice scurrying around).

Morning came and the flight was finally ready to go –
only 24 hours late! When horses fly, they travel in "pallets,"
which look like two horse trailers without the wheels.
However, when the pallets were brought out to start loading
our horses, it became evident that the doors were too small to
fit our horses through. Apparently these pallets had been built
for South American polo ponies, which are much smaller
than our horses. Although we were told to "just squeeze them
through" by the airport officials, our vet was adamant that that
would cause injury. The result was that the pallets were dis-
mantled, the horses were put in, and the airport workers
rebuilt them around the horses. All this took place while elevated on a forklift on the tarmac under the plane with each
rider holding on to the horse with all his or her strength.

After this eventful loading, the flight was good and
we arrived in Argentina safely. Over the next two days, we
increased training time for the horses, all the time monitoring
their temperature and giving them fluids to rehydrate them.
They seemed to be doing well, except that Woody was refusing to eat the Argentinian grain. I spent hours sitting with
him trying to feed him by hand.

By the end of the first team competition day, we had won a bronze medal for Canada! The top-12-placed horses and riders from the team competition move on to compete for individual medals. I was in the unexpected position of not only being the top-placed Canadian but also being tied for fourth overall. I had started the competition hoping to finish in the top 12 but now I had the possibility of winning an individual medal.

On the morning of the individual competition I was very nervous, which was unusual for me as my competition nerves are usually quite good. I busied myself with grooming and braiding Woody. The day was getting hotter and hotter. By the time the competition started it was 35°C and humid. These were very difficult conditions for a horse who only one month earlier had been competing in −25°C weather. On top of that, in competition the riders are expected to wear black hats, black wool coats, and black boots.

I went out to start my warm-up and immediately felt butterflies in my stomach. I looked around the warm-up ring at riders much older and more experienced than me. I continued with the warm-up but felt my concentration slipping. It was extremely hot and at one point all I wanted to do was stop and throw up. My legs were like jelly. I vividly remember that one tree next to the final warm-up ring created an area of shade about 10 metres in diameter. I just wanted to stay in that area of shade.

Just then my coach stopped me and said, "You have two options. You can go in there and ride a safe, clean test and finish in the top 12 or you can go for it." That was all I needed to hear. I turned to my coach and said, "We haven't come all this way just to be in the top 12." Woody and I finished our warm-up and went into the ring. In what seemed like slow motion, Woody and I put in the best performance of our career . . . but was it enough?

As soon as we came out of the ring, we started pouring ice water on Woody to cool him down and, for the first time in my life, I felt my knees buckle as I dismounted. It was now just a waiting game to see if our score would hold up against the last competitors. As the last score came up, my father started leaping in the air – we had won the bronze medal!

After the medal ceremony, the Canadian team held a champagne celebration for all competitors. A wonderful time was had by all – at least it looked that way to me, from the window of the drug-testing station!

VICTORIA WINTER won bronze medals at the North American Dressage Championships in Maryland, 1997, and at the Pan American Games, Mar de Plata, Argentina, 1995.

WARREN SAWKIW

One of my fondest memories of the Olympics doesn't come from any on-field achievement but rather from a friendship I made with a special person, Anke Möhring, a swimmer for the East German team; at that time, East Germany was behind the Iron Curtain.

I quickly found out how important it was that the coaches not see Anke and her teammates in public with me or my friend, Greg O'Halloran. They would be severely reprimanded if they were caught mingling with athletes from democracies like Canada. We found that the best way for us to mingle with them was in the cafeteria after their early morning workouts, or at night, at a common place out in the athletes' village, where no one could see us. We would go for walks communicating in broken English, broken German, and sign language.

Then came the moment I will remember the rest of my life. In the individual swimming medley relay that night, Anke finished third. I can remember the excitement I felt cheering for her to push herself to the finish. After the race she walked by the stands and caught my eye as I waved furiously to get her attention. At that instant I realized that the Olympics are like no other event in the world for they have the ability to break down walls and barriers between countries and religions. For me, the walls between the East and the West had come down, if only for that brief moment.

WARREN SAWKIW was on the Canadian Olympic Team competing in Baseball at the Olympic Games in Seoul, 1988.

TAMAS BUDAY SR.

M y father was my inspiration. Long before I was born, his sport career was behind him and he didn't talk about it much. In the apartment where I grew up with my brothers, a display case with many of his trophies and medals gave silent witness to his past struggles and victories. As a little child I often gazed at his beautiful gold medal from the 1936 Universiade in Italy. I had wild fantasies imagining the particular details of that race. I don't know why, but I never asked

him to tell me the story. Now it is too late and I regret that.
Somehow it was never part of our family discussions. However, the simple presence of the trophies made an impact on
our lives and turned all of us toward sport.

And now, how very proud I am that my three sons have
followed in my footsteps and made the long-term commitment to pursue their Olympic dream.

My chosen sport (and a lifetime love) was the canoe. I was
24 years old when my second son, Tamas, was born. That same
year I won the bronze medal in both the C2 1,000-metre and
the 500-metre events at the 1976 Olympics in Montreal. I
was a Hungarian athlete then and never dreamed that the site
of that race would later play an important role in my life.

Twenty-four years later I was at the same site in Montreal,
this time as Canada's national coach. I was watching the C2
1,000-metre race final unfold. The winner of that race would
represent Canada at the Olympic Games in Sydney. In the
finals were my own two sons, Attila and Tamas. Their goal
was to make the Olympic Team, to go on to match their
father's result, and to bring home a medal.

The competition was very strong. Three weeks earlier at
the trials a younger crew from Nova Scotia had beaten Attila
and Tamas. Over the next three weeks we evaluated that
race and found the areas that could be improved. Higher stroke
rate and a stronger finish combined with smoother boat glide
became the key elements of the plan. Speed, endurance, and
technique were the major elements to focus on, but nutrition,
mental readiness, social support, and relaxation techniques all
got their share of attention.

My toughest day of the year is the team selection day. I
know very well the incredible amount of energy and effort

each athlete puts into his preparation. And yet there is always only one winner. Beside the winner's happy smile, there are the heartbreaking upset and tired faces of the non-winners. The reality of their shattered dreams is so apparent. These days are full of drama. I have to keep neutral and select only the best, based on results, facts, and other specific criteria. My position as national team coach overrules my position as father in this situation. I must be the objective observer and help whoever needs my assistance. I must show respect and decency toward all the participants.

Before the race I wished good luck to all the opponents as well as to my two sons. I left the family support to my youngest son, Peter, and to my wife, Olga. They had come to Montreal just to support the boys. Olga knew how much her presence meant to them. Ever since she was 18, she has been there to support first me and now our boys, even though the excitement is almost too much for her. Three weeks earlier when the boys were defeated, it was Tamas's birthday. Today, it was Mother's Day. A week from now would be her birthday.

I could feel the tension in the air as I stood close to the finish line with a stopwatch in one hand to measure stroke rate, and a video camera in the other. The crowd was surprisingly silent as the race time approached. Then I heard a single strong harsh yell: "Tomiiiiii." It was Peter, standing close to me. He continued his cheering, alternately shouting Attila's and Tamas's names until the race was over. At the end, his voice was gone.

I focused my attention on the small approaching figures. Attila and Tamas were in lane four, and right beside them in lane five was the Nova Scotia crew. There was a straight tailwind on the course, which allowed a higher stroke rate and shorter race time, but also made it harder to breathe. Attila and Tamas settled in for a strong travelling pace after the start. It was critical not to drop that rate. This time they must stay strong enough for the finish. After 500 metres I was able to tell that they had gained more than a boat length's lead over their opponents, but the race was far from over. Both teams increased the tempo. Mike and Richard from Nova Scotia started a long, brave finish. I saw through the camera that their boat was flying at a high speed, running evenly despite the high stroke rate. They continued to creep up to my sons, who were in the lead. With 150 metres to go, only a half boat length separated them. The two boats were far ahead of all the others in this private battle. Tamas and Attila's rate was 67 the last time I measured. Never before had they been able to reach such a high stroke rate at the finish. The nose of their boat was bouncing with each stroke; it wasn't the smoothest glide. "Something to work on later" flashed through my mind. The other crew was pushing hard with an even higher rate and cutting into Attila and Tamas's lead.

At the end, it was a desperate effort from both crews. The question was whether there was enough distance left to catch and change the race position. I turned with the camera as I followed their race. Through it I saw only the two boats with the fighting crews. The two bodies in each boat were united in a powerful synchronized effort. As the angle changed, I saw with a pounding heart that the distance between them had shrunk with each stroke. I could not tell how far there was to go. I just recorded the dramatic fight. Then, both teams kicked their boats forward to the finish line, and the one with a number four was ahead by almost a whole deck. The other crew fell in the water from the great effort. Attila fell back also, but he managed to stay in the boat and did not tip. He lay there, gasping, lacking the strength to move. Tamas as well, paralyzed by lactic acid in his muscles, leaned onto his paddle and with painful little movements maintained the balance for both of them. They didn't move for minutes, too weak to even celebrate. The spectators did it for both crews with grateful applause for a high-quality, spirited race.

After the final check of the boats by the officials, the tension started to relax. Attila and Tamas hugged and congratulated each other, and then Mike and Richard. Tamas was sobbing with emotion. Still too weak to stand on trembling legs, the boys dropped onto the pavement, shaking their heads in disbelief. It was probably the toughest race of their life, and they had done it. When I hugged Tamas and congratulated him, he asked where his mum was. She had disappeared well before the race, to cheer for them in her own private way. Later, Peter and Tamas cried on each other's shoulder, and many of the spectators' eyes were wet with tears also. Finally, when my wife found them, they affectionately hugged each other, and I heard Tamas say, "Happy Mother's Day, Mamata!"

Epilogue: Attila and Tamas raced at the Sydney Olympics but came home without a medal. From their limited funds they paid for the flights to Australia for their mum and their brother, so we could all be together at the Olympic Games. Now they are training hard for the 2004 Olympics. They keep following their dream, and on the way they never lose sight of the values of family and tradition.

TAMAS BUDAY SR. was a double bronze medallist at the Olympic Games in Montreal, 1976, and a four-time World

Champion in 1978, 1981, and 1983. Today he is Canada's National Team Canoe Coach.

TAMAS BUDAY JR.

Dreams are often considered just that – dreams – but when you've been dreaming about one thing since you were young, it can mean more than just a fantasy: it is your life. When I was old enough to understand about the Olympics and learned that my father was a double Olympic bronze medallist, I knew that one day I would follow in his footsteps. From that moment, I cannot remember a time when I did not think it was possible.

TAMAS BUDAY JR. was a member of Canada's Canoe/Kayak Team, Olympic Games, Atlanta, 1996, and Sydney, 2000.

· 16 ·

AT THE HEART OF IT

In 1983 at the age of 16 I had been over the moon when I missed making the National Kayak Team by a 10th of a second. One of the veterans took me aside and told me it was important to have dreams, but that I shouldn't be a dreamer. It has taken me a long time to understand what he meant. Being a dreamer often means you spend more time thinking about something than making it happen. But a dream motivates and compels you to reach your goals.

– David Ford, member of Canada's Canoe/Kayak Team at the Olympic Games, Barcelona, 1992, Atlanta, 1996, Sydney, 2000; World Champion, Spain, 1999

ROBERT IARUSCI

In the summer of 1977 I received a call from Eddie Firmani, the coach of the New York Cosmos, to say I had been purchased from the Toronto Metros-Croatia. I was only 22 years old, and moving to New York and playing among some of the greatest players in the world was an overwhelming proposition. I was going to be a teammate of Pelé, the greatest soccer player who ever played. What was he like? What should I say? How should I act in his presence? What would it be like trying to play alongside him?

He was revered by the world and I wished so badly that he would live up to my expectations of him as a great man as well.

Soon after I joined the team, the Cosmos were playing in Rochester against the Lancers on an August evening. It was the second-last regular-season game, and our opponents were in second place behind us. This game would clinch the top spot for us going into the playoffs. The stadium held only 20,000 people, but on that night there must have been close to 30,000 there, with the overflow sitting on the track in front of the seated areas. Toward the end of every game, Pelé would usually position himself close to the field exit so he could sprint off, avoiding the onslaught of people wanting to touch him.

The game was close, with the Cosmos ahead by the score of 2–1. Pelé was fully engrossed in the match as Rochester was frantically attacking to tie the match. When the final whistle blew, instead of being a few feet from the exit, Pelé found himself in the middle of the park, and it took only a few seconds for the rushing mob to embrace him.

With security and players (I was one of them) forming a protective circle around Pelé, we slowly moved toward the field exit. It was painfully slow because Pelé could not have been more accommodating, always smiling, signing as many autographs as possible. There must have been over a thousand people around us.

As we hit the track, an amazing thing happened. Pelé suddenly stopped and whirled 180 degrees. He put his arms up and stopped everyone in their tracks. He went five deep into the crowd and with the help of security parted the crowd to allow a boy in a wheelchair to come forward. The boy had been waving his right hand, in which he held pencil and paper, in what should have been a hopeless attempt to get the legend's autograph. Pelé went down on one knee, took off his famous number 10 Cosmos jersey, and held it out to the boy. He signed the autograph book and spent about five minutes talking to him and telling the boy that *he* was the real hero in life.

Observing that example of Pelé's humility and learning from it has been a great factor in my own success.

ROBERT IARUSCI was captain of Canada's National Soccer
Team from 1978 to 1984 and was a professional soccer player
in the North American Soccer League from 1975 to 1984.

ELAINE TANNER

On a hot October day in Mexico City, Canada's Olympic
gold medal hopes were pinned on me as I dove into the
water. It was mine to win or lose – the elusive gold was within
my grasp. Little did I know I had much more to lose than just
the gold medal. In a mere one minute and six seconds my life
was to change forever. Not only did I lose the gold when I
touched the end of the pool, but I lost myself . . . my courage
and my confidence.

When I finally did resurface some 20 years later, I came out
with something far more precious than gold. It was not the
kind of gold that would have hung around my neck on that
day in 1968, but the kind that time, grit, and mettle forge from
years of struggle and determination to overcome adversity.

It was a victory that can never be taken away or lost by a
fraction shown on a time clock. Many times our hopes and
dreams can be dashed to pieces in a blink of an eye and our
failures can cut us like swords and leave us to bleed.

It is easy to remain positive and upbeat when we are
successful and winning. The true test comes when we are not.
This is where the true victor shows his or her strength.
Victory, I have learned, needs to be redefined. It is not always
the quickest or most powerful who finish first in life, but the
ones who persevere and remain steadfast within themselves.

The true winner in life struggles to endure and overcome adversities. It is the faith we embrace inside that separates the winners from the losers. No one can defeat us but ourselves.

In my youthful innocence I believed that the Olympic gold would be my ultimate achievement, my crowning glory. Now I know differently.... Our lives are like a book – full of many different chapters. Swimming for me was just one and I have many more to write.

I know to make the most of each page as I write it, and the joy and good that I can include in each sentence makes it all the better. However, when the going gets rough and the words don't come as I hoped they would, I count on my patience, courage, and faith to help me see my way through, knowing the page will always turn in time.

Ironically, in my greatest defeat lay the seeds of my greatest victory! The strength of the human spirit: This in the end is the ultimate achievement and is attainable by all who just have the courage to try.

ELAINE TANNER won two silver medals and a bronze in Swimming at the Olympic Games in Mexico City, 1968, and has won seven Commonwealth Games medals and five Pan American Games titles. She was at the time the youngest recipient of the Order of Canada.

RICK BRANT

I got into competitive running completely by chance, not because of a real passion for the sport. My first memory of running goes back to when I was about four years old. I attended an Alcan-sponsored employee family picnic in Kingston, Ontario. Among the events and festivities offered at the picnic was a fun run for children. I was too young to feel any nervousness. When my father ushered me to the starting line, he told me to run as fast as I could to the finish line. I did and won the race.

A photographer at the picnic took a picture of me winning the race. The next day it appeared in the local newspaper, and I became an instant celebrity (at least to my family). That was the first point in my life that I became aware of my ability to run.

Throughout my elementary school years in Kingston, I was always the fastest in my grade, winning all the red ribbons for running at our annual field day. However, my dream was to become an NHL hockey player, so my energies were focused on playing hockey. It was a struggle because I didn't possess the natural skills that others seemed to have. By the time I was 15, I was living in Ottawa and although I had made it to the highest levels of minor hockey, I had come to the realization that I certainly wasn't going to make it to the NHL. Out of frustration and disappointment I was ready to give up hockey.

In high school I continued to excel in running, always finishing near the top at our mandatory school-wide annual cross-country race. Because of my modest success, some teachers and students tried to convince me to try out for the school's track and field and cross-country teams. I declined. I simply had no interest. However once I made the decision to quit hockey, I realized I needed to redirect my energies, so I decided to give running a chance – more out of boredom than anything else. That spring I made the track team, came second at each of the local and regional meets, and made it to the Ontario Championships, where I won a bronze medal in the 800 metres.

In spite of my successes, I was struggling to find my motivation for running. Training was okay, but I hated doing the mileage necessary to excel in the sport. One day, I think to try to encourage me to invest in the sport the time that it required, my father told me of two unique opportunities. The first related to a one-mile foot race held on our reserve (Tyendinaga Mohawk Territory). In addition to receiving money, the winner's name was engraved on a large trophy that permanently resided at the Council Office. If anyone won the race for three consecutive years, he would get to keep the trophy. In the long history of the event, few had ever achieved this honour. The second opportunity was the Tom Longboat Award, a national award given annually to the most outstanding First Nations athlete in Canada. I knew nothing of the individual the award was named after, so my father shared with me what he knew of Tom Longboat, the legendary Onondaga runner who, at the beginning of the 20th century, was the world's champion distance runner.

The opportunity to win such awards intrigued me. Although running a mile was significantly longer than the distances I typically raced, I was confident that with some added training I could do well enough to win. As far as the Longboat Award, I dismissed it as unattainable.

This brief conversation with my father marked a significant turning point. His comments started me on a journey of self-reflection. I started to realize that there was a rich legacy of First Nations runners and I wanted to know how my gift or abilities and ancestral heritage might relate to what

Longboat and other notable First Nations runners had done before me.

I looked into Longboat's career and wrote an essay on him for one of my classes at school. Studying the incredible accomplishments of this athlete helped me to develop a greater appreciation for the sport and my own heritage. I now saw myself as not just a person of First Nations ancestry but a First Nations runner.

I had found my focus. I asked my father to enter me into the Tyendinaga foot race. Although by then I had competed at provincial and national track meets, I wasn't prepared for the atmosphere of the race. It was a community spectacle, a throwback to the days when foot racing was the highlight of country fairs. All the activities stopped as the announcer proclaimed over the PA system that the event was about to begin. Spectators gathered around the fence to watch the race, which was run around the old horse race track – a far cry from the modern synthetic tracks that I normally trained and competed on. And rather than an anonymous group of people sitting in the bleachers watching a track meet, it was my people, Mohawk people, cheering all the competitors on. At that moment, nerves and all, I remember feeling a great sense of belonging.

I won that race and continued to do so for three consecutive years. It was those very simple, grassroots experiences that helped to solidify my commitment to running. It served to establish a sense of self-awareness and pride for my Mohawk roots and a connection to my God-given ability to run. I had found my motivation and developed a passion for the sport that I had always struggled to appreciate.

Four years later, while I was training and competing on

the West Coast, I received a call to say that I had been selected as the national recipient of the 1987 Tom Longboat Award.

In front of hundreds of chiefs from across Canada, who were attending the Assembly of First Nations' Conference in Edmonton, Alberta, I was presented the award by Tom Longboat Jr. In his speech, he acknowledged my achievements by reflecting on his father's passion for running – the passion of the great Iroquois runner who had done so much to inspire me.

RICK BRANT was a member of Canada's Track and Field Team from 1986 to 1988. Since his departure from competitive running, he has worked in support of Aboriginal sport development across Canada.

IAN SOELLNER

During the Barcelona Olympics I had finished my event (pentathlon) early and had the final week and a half to enjoy the games as a spectator.

My teammate was competing in another sport, and I was late as usual getting down to the fencing venue to cheer him on. As I rushed down the stairs from our apartment in the athletes' village, I nearly ran over the athlete living next door to us. After apologizing, I asked her how her event was going and she replied, "Well, I am very happy with the way I competed." I found it strange that she had competed well enough to satisfy herself but still seemed so sad. She didn't seem to want to talk much more about it and I was late so I left it at that and ran to catch the Metro. When I arrived home at the village that evening, I learned about the controversy that was unfolding.

Sylvie Fréchette had lost the gold medal because of a technical error made by one of the judges. Then I understood how she could be happy with the way she had competed but still be so very sad. The greatest thing I took home with me from the Barcelona Olympics, apart from seeing first-hand the tremendous sportsmanship of Sylvie, was the knowledge that if you are happy with the effort you have given, then nothing else matters.

IAN SOELLNER competed in Modern Pentathlon at the Olympic Games in Barcelona, 1992. At the Modern Pentathlon Pan American Championships, he was a silver medallist in 1994 and bronze medallist in 1997.

SYLVIE FRÉCHETTE

My mother used to tell me everything happens for a reason. Often such sentiments go in one ear and out the other. And even though I thought, "Yeah, yeah, yeah!" the saying must have stuck with me because I'm logical – I knew from synchronized swimming that if you move to the left, it's because of what your right arm is doing. Although you can't always apply that kind of logic to real-life events, I tried. I tried especially to make sense of two events that happened to me in 1992.

The events were the suicide of my fiancé, Sylvain Lake, and an error in the entering of my marks at the Olympic

Games in Barcelona. I had found Sylvain at our place just five days before I was to leave for the Olympics. In spite of the terrible shock and sadness, I had decided to go ahead with the competition.

When I got out of the pool after my compulsory figures, I knew I had put in a top performance and was expecting to see numbers reflecting that. I could scarcely believe it when my numbers showed I had come in second. No matter how well I swam in the final, I would not win the gold. It didn't help that there was a rational explanation – the Brazilian judge had entered an incorrect number by mistake and in spite of protests from the Canadian team it was decided that it would not be rectified. For a full day I could not bring myself to believe what had happened.

When I came back from the Olympic Games in Barcelona, thousands of people were at the airport to welcome me home. Their support motivated me after what had been a painful and traumatic few weeks: I decided I was going to live my life to the full – "Watch me go" became my motto. It lasted for a year and then I crashed. The body is the most beautiful machine in the world but you have to look after it.

In the weeks and months after the Olympics, I had been giving motivational speeches in which I emphasized the importance of having a dream – but my own dream was gone. In my speeches I was talking about the past, about the dream I used to have. I avoided questions about the future. Driving home from these appearances, I would be in tears, full of self-pity and thinking "Poor little Sylvie." I also felt I was deceiving my audiences – *I* knew I was a loser and didn't have a dream but I was acting as if everything was still okay. It was clear something was missing so I returned to the only thing I

knew how to do – swimming competitively. I came out of
retirement and made my goal going to the Olympics. I
qualified for the team and went to Atlanta. But even after
winning the silver medal, I felt I was back at square one.

Finally a friend said to me, "You need to see someone, a
therapist, a psychiatrist." She gave me a phone number and
said, "This woman is not the sweet little thing she seems.
She'll make you find your own solutions." For a while I put
off going but one day, on the way home from a tour, I called
on her at her house in the country. She didn't really know
much about me, for which I was thankful. The important
thing in her view was that I was ready to make a commitment
to deal with my depression.

For a year and a half, I saw her. Every time I went to her
house, she'd tell me to turn off my cell phone. Take your shoes
off and walk on the earth, she'd say. Feel the wind. She would
start by making me work in her garden – thinning beets,
carrots, that sort of thing. She made me breathe, listen to the
wind, even listen to the chickens. She would feed me her
homemade yogurt and make me salad from her own garden.
It would take about half an hour to get me grounded, then I
was ready to talk.

It was a scary process. She helped me discover I was using
my fiancé's suicide and what had happened at Barcelona as dis-
tractions from dealing with other sadnesses of my life. When
she had asked me to talk about myself, I talked about these
recent events but she said, "No – who are *you*? Who is *Sylvie*?"

So I went back to the time I was a child and right up to
the Olympics. I started with my father, who had died when I
was three and a half. I don't remember him clearly but I have

flashes of him. He was a bus driver and he would leave home early in the morning. My bedroom was in the kitchen and he would wake me up in the morning. I would sit on his knee while he fed me steak and potatoes. Before he went to work, he would put me back to bed. I told the therapist what I could remember. She said, "Sylvie, you need to say 'Goodbye Daddy.'" I couldn't do it. I started to cry.

It was hard, but I found a way to say goodbye to my father. I realized there was no tombstone at his grave. So my way of saying goodbye was to put up a tombstone. Now I go there whenever I can – I have taken my husband there to introduce him to my father and will introduce him to my daughter when she is born.

Today, eight or nine years later, when I look back I still don't understand the reasons for the things that happened, but I've learned it's important to deal with traumatic events in order to move on with life. People still write to me about what happened that summer but I want them to take hope from my story because I'm not poor little Sylvie any more. I'm proud of who I have become, the real Sylvie.

SYLVIE FRÉCHETTE was awarded the silver medal in Synchronized Swimming at the Olympic Games in Barcelona, 1992, but in 1993, the judge's error was rectified and she received her gold medal. She was a silver medallist at the Olympic Games in Atlanta, 1996.

LARRY CAIN

Ever since I'd won gold and silver medals in canoeing at the 1984 Olympics in Los Angeles, I'd been looking forward to taking another run at the Olympic podium. My training in the 1986–87 season was more thorough than it had ever been and despite a disappointing sixth-place finish at the World Championships in 1987 I was paddling faster than ever and had been successful in international regattas. I was fitter, stronger, more experienced, and definitely ready to mount the podium in Seoul.

I breezed through the Olympic trials, got off to a solid start in June, and had tremendous results in July. Heading into the month before the Olympics I knew two things: I was faster than I had ever been and I was stronger in 1,000 metres than 500 metres.

When we got to Seoul I had a few outstanding workouts, but more and more I had workouts that felt flat. Before long, I was fearing I had left my best paddling for the year behind me. Could the excitement and enthusiasm I carried with me all year have led me to do too much too soon? Could my constant effort to squeeze just a little more speed out of my paddling have caused me to overtrain? Could we have made a mistake in the preparation?

In addition, on the first day of competition, my heat in the 500 metres was cancelled. Some athletes had withdrawn at the last minute and as luck would have it they were all from my heat! It was decided everyone in my heat would advance to the semifinal. I didn't want to race in a semi without having had the heat to work the bugs out but I had no choice.

The next day I easily qualified for the semi of the 1,000

metres and left the course looking forward to the 500-metre semi on day three. All it took that morning was a shaky start. I'd been able to recover from a start like that many times before, so I was confident I could come in the top three and thus make the final. There is no time to look around in a 500-metre sprint so I just put my head down and cranked it up. I can still remember the feeling of shock when I hit the finish line and realized I had come fourth. It was close, but I was definitely fourth. I was devastated. I was the defending Olympic champion and now I wasn't even a finalist.

In a daze I put my boat away and got changed. Still shaken, I went back to the village. That afternoon I must have thrown a thousand paper airplanes off the roof of our apartment. The more planes I made and launched, the more it seemed the disappointment of the morning was being carried away with each plane. I had the semifinal of my better event coming up tomorrow. After a couple of hours of airplanes, I found myself looking ahead and not back. I couldn't wait to get back to the course for the 1,000-metre semi on day four.

The semi on day four was good. Not outstanding – it didn't have to be – but it was solid. I felt strong and confident. I was in the final!

Day five brought one of the hardest things I have had to do in sport – watch the 500-metre final. As I watched the race come down the course, I could feel myself consumed by hunger to make the most of the one chance I had left.

Day six. October 1, 1988. I got up at 6:30 a.m. and went to the cafeteria for breakfast. It was cold and pitch black. I remember seeing the tiny girls on the East German gymnastics team, having already finished their competition, leaving the buffet counters with plates loaded with bacon and eggs,

pancakes, sausages, hash browns, and fresh fruit only to have
their stern-looking coach scrape most of it off. I quietly had
my breakfast and went back to my room to get my things to
head for the course.

On shore I got some last-minute words of advice and luck
from my coaches, Jim Reardon and Tamas Buday, and some
teammates. I placed my number on my boat and made a final
check of my boat to make sure everything was secure, and
with Jim and Tamas at my side I picked up my boat and went
to the dock. Then I was on my own as I pushed off. I felt good
– strong and hungry and ready. I paddled slowly up the return
lane. As I turned my boat around and entered my lane, I could
feel the headwind, which was very strong and kicking up a
light chop. I figured the main threat in the race would come
from Ivan Klementiev of the U.S.S.R., who was on the other
side of the course to my left, and Jorg Schmidt from East
Germany, who was to my immediate right. I centred my boat
in my lane and got the angle I felt I needed for the start. It was
tough to keep the angle in the wind and it felt like the starter
was holding us for an unusually long time, but it didn't bother
me. I took a few deep breaths, relaxed, and looked down my
lane to wait for the start command.

"Attention, please!" The starter's voice broke the silence.
"Bang!" The start gun! We were off. My start felt solid and
strong. The wind was really strong, even stronger than I
thought it was going to be, but I like headwinds. At 400 metres
I took my first glimpse of the field. Klementiev was way in
front. Schmidt was clearly second and I was clearly third.
Nobody else in the field was close. I had been training all year,
with great success, at building the pace at 500 metres with a
commitment to dynamic, snappy strokes. If I did it right, my

stroke rate would rise by only one or two strokes a minute but my boat speed would increase. My stroke felt a little heavier than I liked at 500 metres, and although I could feel I was pulling away from the field, Schmidt still seemed to be slowly pulling away from me.

At 700 metres, my stroke still wasn't as light as I'd wanted, but I wasn't dying. Through the 750-metre mark! In this headwind there were probably about 65 seconds left. I went through the 800-metre mark. Time to put everything into going for the finish! I wasn't going to catch Schmidt today, that was clear. I probably wasn't going to catch Klementiev either. But I could come third. The last strokes were painful. I could feel my muscles failing. I crossed the line and immediately looked to my left to see where Klementiev was. He'd won, by a lot, and Schmidt to my right had come second. What I couldn't believe was that the Bulgarian, Nikolai Buchalov, was sitting back in his boat to Klementiev's immediate left and appeared to be third. Where had he come from?

We headed immediately to the boat control dock. As I took each easy stroke to the dock, I prayed that somehow I had been able to hold Buchalov off. The results were coming up on the scoreboard as I stepped onto the dock. I was fourth. I let the officials take my boat to weigh it and I sat down on the far end of the dock and cried. The dream of getting back on the podium was over, I had failed by the narrowest of margins. I was familiar with the feeling of disappointment – I'd come fourth twice at the World Championships – but that didn't make it any easier to take.

I don't remember taking my boat back to the boathouse, putting it away, or packing up my equipment. I don't remember the words I exchanged with my coaches, Jim and Tamas.

I remember being up in the stands watching the rest of the finals and getting handshakes and congratulations from my teammates and hugs from my family.

As I dealt with the press, I'm sure I let my disappointment show. However I refused to feel sorry for myself or be cornered into saying I had "choked." I knew I had put together the best race I could have that day. I had raced tactically well. I felt solid but my stroke had felt heavier than I liked. I knew I hadn't been racing with my best form. I thought back to the words of my first coach, Bill Collins, who had helped instill a competitive spirit in me. He said that in a race "if you can't win, you fight like hell to come second. If you can't come second, you do everything you can to come third. If you can't come third, you scratch and claw to come fourth. If you can't come fourth . . ." I had given everything I could and come fourth. It would take a long time to get over the disappointment of that but I had earned the right to hold my head high. That night I went out on the town with my teammates and friends and somewhere along the way they presented me with an "aluminum medal" made from the top of a beer can for my fourth-place finish. I still have that aluminum medal today.

I learned a lot about myself and sport through my Seoul experience. I learned that I could perform well under pressure despite not having my best form. I learned how to deal with some of the most bitter disappointments and compete the next day without it affecting my performance. I appreciated the significance of my Los Angeles medals more after Seoul. My hat will always go off to athletes who come close even if their results go largely unrecognized by those who applaud medals.

In the grand scheme of things the difference between the bronze medal and my fourth means little to me now. Before I left the course in Seoul for the last time, one of my teammates, Hugh Fisher, himself an Olympic champion, took me aside to say he had bad news. While we had been racing, one of our former teammates had been killed in a helicopter crash in British Columbia. It seemed silly that I had been crying over missing a medal when a family in Canada was crying over the loss of a son, a brother, a husband, and a father.

This news, combined with my own experience in Seoul, helped me put sport in perspective.

LARRY CAIN was a gold and silver medallist in Canoeing at the Olympic Games in Los Angeles, 1984, and a member of the Canadian Olympic Team in Seoul, 1988, and Barcelona, 1992.

· 17 ·

A CHILD'S GIFT

After winning a silver medal in Los Angeles in 1984, I had a tremendous letdown in Seoul, Korea, in 1988. On my leg of the relay I dropped the baton after getting bumped by a runner coming around a turn. When the CBC tried to interview me, my answers were buried under my incessant crying. In addition, the Ben Johnson situation and ensuing drug scandal left the formerly close and united Canadian track team in tatters, ending a memorable era in Canadian sport.

I found it difficult to pick up my life and move on. I left the track world and found work as a teaching assistant for special needs kids. They were a challenge and I wasn't sure if I was cut out for the work – until I met an eight-year-old, partially autistic boy named Stephen. I'd been told not to waste my time with him but I didn't listen.

The staff often found the best way to encourage many of the children was to offer a reward. If you wanted them to read a book or do their math you would promise a cookie or another treat. But when, for fun, I introduced Stephen to the world of track and field, he no longer needed promises or rewards. He took to it better than any other student – you only had to show him an activity once. Hurdles and high jump were no problem for the little boy who had trouble sitting at a desk for more than five minutes at a time. I loved the smile Stephen wore at the track. The obvious joy he experienced there made me realize I was doing something far more important than winning silver medals and worrying about dropping batons.

– Molly Killingbeck, silver medallist, Canadian Track and Field Team, Olympic Games, Los Angeles, 1984; gold medallist at the Commonwealth Games, Brisbane, 1982, and Edinburgh, 1986

PETER FONSECA

Toronto, eastern standard time: 7:30 a.m.
Date: February 8, 1992
Forecast: -12 degrees Celsius
Location: Pearson International Airport: I am about to board
Flight 324 – Air Canada to San Juan, Puerto Rico

"But I specifically called ahead to make sure that I had a
window seat. I'm running a very important race in a few days,
and I need to sleep on this flight."

Occupation: Professional distance runner, who must always
be focused on himself

The San Blas Half-Marathon is a race that brings runners
from all over the world to compete for a large purse and
is a perfect tune-up before a major spring marathon. The
town of Coamo, Puerto Rico, has organized this international event for the past 50 years. With its 40,000 people, it has
built the event into one of the most important stops on the
international circuit for distance runners.

I had competed in this race for the past three years with a best place of seventh and was hoping to better this significantly this season. The organization had always treated me extremely well. This year, the race organizer, Miguel Cerón, had asked if I would be willing to do a training workshop with the kids from the local track club. My first concern was how this two-hour session would affect *my* race, *my* energy level, *my* performance. Feeling that the heat and humidity would drain me, I was reluctant to be out under the scorching sun and blanketing humidity for so long.

However, with so many years of support from Miguel, I was compelled to give the talk.

Coamo, Puerto Rico, 2:15 p.m.
Forecast: 31 degrees Celsius, 92% humidity
Location: Local track club

I step out of my chauffeured, air-conditioned car, wearing my $200 running shoes, $100 shorts and T-shirt, and all the rest of the running paraphernalia that I get paid by my sponsors to wear. Immediately 50 local boys and girls surround me. They bombard me with questions about Canada, snow, the Blue Jays, girlfriends, running, travelling, and how I like Puerto Rico. We are laughing and playing before I begin to give them a simple workshop on the mechanics of distance running.

It is at this point that I begin to notice that many of the kids are not even wearing shoes. Some have old worn-out shoes, and many are wearing tattered T-shirts and shorts. Soon I forget about time and stop worrying about how this little talk may affect *my* race, *my* performance, *myself.* One hour turns into two, into four, and soon dusk is upon us. I have had an amazing day and find myself sad to go.

As I gather my things, a young boy comes up to me. Taking his shirt off, he extends his arms with gratitude. This young boy who has so little, and I am sure very few clothes in his closet, is giving his shirt to me. I am overwhelmed; this is a complete act of selflessness. I am speechless. I shake my head and say, "No, I can't accept something that I know you need so much." The boy insists and I accept his gift with much admiration. The only thing I can do in return is take my shirt off and hand it to him.

How did the race go? I ended up finishing 11th. Not as good as I had hoped for. However, of all the many races I have run and places I have been to around the world, with all the prize money and personal success, I can say that this one moment of selflessness by a young boy taught me more than any other experience. I set out seeking personal gratification when I went to talk in the village. In the end, I received one hundred fold in return.

PETER FONSECA is a marathon runner who was on the Canadian Olympic Team in Atlanta, 1996, and was the top-ranked Canadian marathoner for seven years.

CHARMAINE CROOKS

Sometimes events happen in your life that leave a lasting impression. This was one of those life-changing times. In 1994 I was competing at the Commonwealth Games in

Victoria, British Columbia. There had been a postcard campaign across Canada during the Games encouraging kids to send letters to Canadian athletes. I received many letters from school children but one letter stood out from the rest. It read, "Win a melad Charmaine" and was signed by a six-year-old child, Caleb Currie, who lived in Creston, British Columbia.

After I won my "melad" – a silver in the 800 metres, which was a real surprise to me considering I was recovering from an ankle injury – I was being interviewed on television by Brian Williams. Just before the interview, I asked if I could bring the letter from Caleb to say hi to him and also to show the troll that my eight-year-old niece had given me for good luck. He agreed.

During the interview I showed Brian the card. While the camera was getting a close-up view, I said "hello" to Caleb and showed off my lucky troll.

After I returned to my home in Vancouver following the Commonwealth Games, I was getting ready one day to go to the airport to compete in Europe. Just before leaving my home, I went to check my mail and there waiting for me was a letter from a teacher at Caleb's school.

It was a letter I will never forget. It explained that Caleb had been killed on his way to school one morning as he was riding his bicycle. The teacher thanked me very much for showing Caleb's card on TV because he had been so excited to see it and hear me say hello. She explained that this had been a school project – following the progress of an athlete – and every day Caleb would run home from school just to hear about my results on the radio and television. It had meant a great deal to him to be remembered and thanked.

I got in touch with his family and still have a picture of him that they gave to me.

It was one of those moments that touched my life forever. I realized as never before how much the smallest gesture can mean to a child and how much impact we all can have on the lives of children. Holding up the card and mentioning his name had seemed to me so simple yet it meant so much to Caleb.

I still have the letter from the teacher as a reminder that these seemingly insignificant actions can make a world of difference – and just when I feel so tired and wonder how I can go to another school talk or autograph session, I remember how energized I become by the children I meet. And any time a child asks me for something – I remember Caleb.

CHARMAINE CROOKS was an Olympic silver medallist in Athletics at the Olympic Games in Los Angeles, 1984, and a member of Canada's Olympic Team at the Olympic Games in Moscow, 1980 (boycotted Games), Seoul, 1988, Barcelona, 1992, and Atlanta, 1996. She was a Commonwealth and Pan American Games gold medallist. She was elected as a Member of the International Olympic Committee's Athletes' Commission and devotes her time within the sport community both nationally and internationally.

BILL TRAYLING

"Three minutes to start!"
I heard the starter's call to approach the line at the 1984 Olympic Trials for kayak. I was ready. I was focused.

"Deep breath, Bill. Squeeze the paddle – relax the arms – feel the power in my ability." I ignored the freezing cold wind on my bare knuckles as I circled slowly toward the start line.

"One minute to start!"

I pulled into the starting block and looked down the 500-metre course. I recalled a fleeting thought. In a brief attempt to psyche me up, the National Team coach had told me I only needed to finish third to make the team. I had already defeated everyone in the race easily in the heats. This was to be my day, what I'd spent three months in training camp – and five long years – training for.

It was all about to come together . . . .

But instead, my entire existence came apart with every stoke after an uneventful first 250 metres. The last 20 metres would make their indelible mark as the most painful of my life. In 10 seconds, I fell from first to fifth place. As I reached the finish line, I was barely moving forward. As I struggled to move my arms, I heard my coach from the shoreline: "Oh Bill . . . oh, Bill, no."

I didn't make the team. I didn't fulfil my dream. I choked.

As I tied my wet kayak to the roof rack on my car, my father approached, forcing a smile. His weary eyes showed the fatigue from the radiation and the chemotherapy. I continued to tie down my boat. I wondered if things could be worse.

The team was announced in a little room crowded with excited families. Itineraries were handed out and the plan for the team was discussed. I sat there with my friend Chris, and we "small-talked" while others revelled in their success. The coach approached gingerly and told me that I was his first alternate if anyone was needed in L.A. I nodded a weak thank you and stared over his shoulder as people I'd defeated for years hugged in celebration.

Sitting on the bed in my hotel room, I watched TV with the sound off. The beer in my hand was getting warm as I fiddled with the foil label. A few guys stopped by the room to see me. As they did I motioned to the other bed where my father slept. He was trying to get some rest before we hit the highway for home. It was good to see him sleep. I thought of the three hours I'd been up with him the night before as he screamed in pain. He'd been sleeping in his own room at home so he wouldn't keep my mum up at night. I wondered if I'd have been smarter to have taken my own room in the hotel as he had wanted. No – with his level of pain I wasn't going to leave him alone. He had made the trip to see his son make the Olympic Team. I was going to be there for him as we both tried to sleep the night before the race.

As I drove out of Montreal, my eyes felt heavy. I looked over at my father as he slept in the passenger seat. I turned the volume on the radio up a bit to keep me awake. He opened his eyes, cleared his throat, and whispered five words: "I'm proud of you, son."

I drove on, silent tears flowing. I realized that although I had failed to make the Olympic Team, I had succeeded in a much greater way. I was my father's son. That's all I had to be.

"Next time, Dad. Next time . . ."

We buried my father four months later on a beautiful September afternoon.

In the months between the trials and that day, I rallied and provided some controversy as I defeated Olympic Team members at the National Championships – with my father watching from his hospital bed. I won six medals at that

Nationals, all of which I buried with my dad. He and I cheered together as Larry Cain, our family friend, won Olympic gold for Canada in the C1 500 metres. I believe that Larry gave my father a few extra weeks of life by coming to the house and placing his Olympic gold medal around his neck.

Three weeks after my father's funeral I had reconstructive surgery on my shoulder. As 1984 ended, I resumed training with a new four-year focus. In 1985 I moved to the front of the line with the National Team. My team finished ninth at the World Championships in fours, and I was third in Canada in singles. In 1986, the good times continued as I retained my spot in the K4 and raced hard at home as we hosted the Worlds in Montreal. I finished off the year with a silver medal at the Commonwealth Championships. I was on track for Seoul in 1988, my mother supporting me, driven by the memory of my father and the promise of "next time."

We won the first set of 1988 Olympic trials, in Toronto. Our crew of four only had to repeat the victory at the second trials in two weeks, and we'd be on the plane to Seoul.

One more race. One more victory. "Next time" was now.

"One minute to start – please approach the start line!"

Here it was – the dream about to become reality. We approached the line. It was just us and them – two crews – and "they" knew what we had achieved two weeks earlier. As I set the nose of the boat on the line between the lane markers, the wind blew us fiercely to the right. I looked to the starter and raised my paddle to signal that we were crooked and not ready, a common action in trials races situations.

The official nodded. As I attempted to draw the bow of the boat sideways, I heard words I will never forget –

"Attention please!" – I could not believe it! He had fired the gun before I was ready!

Our first ten strokes were terrible. By the time we regained our composure we were almost a length behind. Through the entire three-minute, 1,000-metre race, we came back, inch by inch, but in the end it was not enough. We finished eight inches behind the other crew – tied in the race to the Olympics. We were incensed, devastated, blown away. Why had the starter not waited?

As we approached the dock, our families stood in shock. I sat on the dock for a long time, thinking of my dad. I had failed to keep my promise. "Next time" was slipping away.

I thought, "One more chance to do it right." We had another two weeks to prepare for the final selection race in Montreal. The course there had been good to me after that haunting cold day in 1984.

Two weeks later we raced in Montreal. We raced our best. We lost.

This was "next time" and it didn't feel like it was supposed to feel.

Failure this time was much more painful. This was not a 20-year-old newcomer choking under the pressure of a dying father. This was four years of expectation, four years of sacrifice while my peers retired to real life. This was the "next time" that would never be. It was over. I was done.

I retired from the team after the National Championships that year. I was bitter and wanted to be as far away from the sport as I could get. It was more than a year before I wandered into the Mississauga Canoe Club, where I had started racing as a 13-year-old.

As I sat by the river, I was approached by a man who

recognized my Canada jacket. He was waiting for his daughter, who had just taken up the sport. He asked me to talk to her because she was nervous about her upcoming competition.

I waited for the young paddler on the dock I had pushed off from so many times – in the heat, in the cold, in the rain, in the snow. As the little girl attempted to lift her boat from the water, I noticed it was the same boat I had raced in at my first Nationals. "Do you know how old that boat is?" I asked. "Nope," she said. "Well, it's about the same age as you!" She looked at me – the way only a nine-year-old can!

The ensuing conversation was to change my outlook forever.

"Why do you paddle?" I asked.

"'Cuz it's fun!" she explained.

"What is the most fun about it?"

"I like the friends I meet," she quickly replied. As I helped carry her boat to the drying racks, she asked me who I was. I told her and said I'd been on the National Team. She asked, "Did you go to the Olympics?"

I paused . . . and a lump began to swell in my throat. "No, I didn't," I replied. "I raced for eleven years and travelled all over the world though." Then she looked up at me and asked the question that changed my direction from that day forward. "Did you have fun?"

As I look back, it was that talk that set my mind on a new road. It was the realization that my dream as a young paddler, too, had been simply to enjoy things. The first day, and even the first year of my paddling life was driven by a desire to make friends and have fun. And I did.

That day I re-evaluated the promise I had made to my father: to make the team "the next time" I had the chance.

True – I had not made the Olympic Team but I made three World Championship Teams from 1985 to 1987. Now it was time to help others make the teams of their choice and fulfil their dreams. There would be many more "next times" as I built a reputation for myself as a coach and leader.

That talk with the little girl and the promise to my father were foremost on my mind when I hosted the send-off to Sydney for our club's three Olympic athletes in 2000. It was my sixth successful year as the head coach of the club, having won four National Club Championships. We had also put six athletes on the 1992, 1996, and 2000 Olympic Teams. That day, a particular young woman stood ready to accept the small plaque the club was awarding to each of our Olympians.

It was the little girl I had spoken to.

I was immensely proud. Families and friends congratulated her and the two boys who were to travel to Sydney with her. These boys themselves had carried my boat to the water at the 1988 trials. Now they were men going to their second Olympic Games. As each of them spoke, they thanked me for leading the club they had grown up at. And publicly, that day, for the first time, I thanked my father for giving me the opportunity to realize that there is always another next time, if you create it.

BILL TRAYLING was a member of the Canadian Canoe/ Kayak Team from 1982 to 1988. He is in his sixth year as the head coach of the 15-time National Champion Mississauga Canoe Club.

· 18 ·

SO PROUD! SO PROUD!

*It was our first time wearing the red maple leaf on our backs
. . . the dream of every curler, young and old, male or female,
tall or short, graceful or klutzy. Because to wear the red and
white at the Olympics meant you had triumphed as a
Canadian champion.*

– George Karrys, Olympic silver medallist, Canadian Men's
Curling Team, Olympic Winter Games, Nagano, 1998

SANDRA McCAIG

In the summer, if the wind is up, you can see them out there skimming the far horizon – "catching the wind." Chances are you may be watching one of the McCaig siblings: Amy, Olympic hopeful, or her brother Kelly or her brother Murray. Their father calls them the Prairie sequence – their sails flashing Can 7, Can 8, and Can 9 – all with dreams of representing Canada at the Olympics. For the McCaig siblings, windsurfing has been a family venture. They have been sailing the lake some 15 years now in search of the Olympic Dream.

All three children have been Canadian champions, and the ocean has been their competitive playground. They have lived and trained around the world, each with hopes of becoming the one sailor to represent Canada at the Olympics in the sport of windsurfing. They have trained together in the summer on Lake Winnipeg at the family cottage and, when the lake froze over in the winter, travelled to warmer climes to set up training camps. They have competed with those who live year-round by the ocean and who are amazed that a sailor could be born and bred on the Prairies.

For the last 15 years I have watched each child in turn mount an Olympic campaign and leave home in pursuit of a dream. I cried when my first son left home at 20, my second at 18, and my daughter at 17. Theirs has often been a lonely pursuit, in distant lands, and often with great adventure and at personal cost. I have seen firsthand their successes and failures. I have celebrated in joy and commiserated in sorrow. My husband has been at command central when planes have been missed, passports stolen, credit cards lost, equipment broken, and sails left behind. He has been their personal manager and fundraiser, exceeded his credit limit, written hundreds of letters for corporate support, and driven them to an even greater number of racing events. I cheered on the sidelines and pasted all their news clippings in scrapbooks.

I have been a personal psychologist and sounding board, hugging my son after his accident, consoling another when he was injured, and weeping with my daughter when she lost the Olympic trials. I have watched them with fear in my heart as they sailed alone on angry seas and worried about them being attacked by sharks in foreign waters. My stomach has knotted tightly as I've watched them compete, often against each other. Each summer I have anxiously awaited their return from winter training.

I have seen my children grow and mature and develop skills and extensive knowledge through their sport. They have been afforded great opportunities to learn about life on an international scene and acquire a global understanding. I have watched them proudly as the Canadian flag slowly unfurled while the national anthem played in their honour. I always smile when I see the Olympic rings tattooed on Murray's shoulder.

I have learned that youth from around the world have the same hopes, aspirations, and values. I have learned about the power of a dream, personal mission, goal-setting, and commitment. After seeing what my children have accomplished and who they have become, I now believe that indeed "anything is possible when you have a dream." After all, who would have thought a windsurfer from the Prairies? And what advice have I to give to others on a "quest for gold"? Set no limits. Live your dreams!

SANDRA McCAIG is the mother of windsurfers Murray McCaig, Kelly McCaig, and Amy McCaig. The McCaigs are the most successful family in Canadian Windsurfing history. At least one of the three siblings has represented Canada on the National Team since 1988.

ROB SNOEK

I was probably the shortest high jumper in the competition that day.

It was the district track and field meet at the Civic Fields in Oshawa, Ontario. I was in Grade 8, and I was exactly five feet tall.

I wasn't incredibly confident going into this event. I had only made it to this level once before – in Grade 6 – and I had *never* won a ribbon. In fact, my real goal when the track and field season began was to make the team. It came as a bit of a surprise to me, and everyone else, when I qualified first from our school and thus would go to the *big* field day.

It was a hot day in June. The high jump wasn't the first event so I watched some of my friends and schoolmates compete and started to get excited, and nervous. I really can't remember what kind of warm-up routine I had but it certainly wasn't very elaborate.

The first round is always the hardest. No one wants to fail at the opening height. I cleared the bar and started to feel less nervous as the adrenaline took over.

There were at least 20 high jumpers in the field so it took a while between jumps. Eventually, as the bar was raised, some boys started to fail and the field got smaller and smaller. I had some difficulty at a couple of fairly low heights and it took me more than one attempt to clear the bar (each athlete gets three tries at each height). I was kind of mad at myself because I knew I could do better.

At one point during the competition the official for the event (who of course was a teacher) read the names of the athletes who remained. I realized there were only seven left and I was one of them. And then there were five. Wow, I was in the top five.

After the next height, I was one of only three competitors left. I would go home with a ribbon that day. That was an awesome feeling.

Before the next round I studied my competitors. Both were taller than me. One was big and strong and looked like he might be ready to shave soon. The other was lean and looked, um, like a high jumper. Oh well, I thought, at least I would get a ribbon – third place is okay.

But then something strange happened. We all failed on all three attempts at the next height. A jump-off was necessary, kind of like overtime in other sports where the next one to clear the bar wins.

I prepared for my jump by staring at the bar. I was trying to convince my body that it could make it over. I rubbed my fingers together – ever so lightly – trying to feel "as light as a feather." I ran towards the bar and planted my right foot . . .

Sometimes, as a high jump event progresses, it can draw a crowd because it's dramatic and fun to watch. That was the case this day. In fact, it may have been drawing a larger crowd than usual because rumours had started to spread that one of the contenders in the senior boys' high jump had an artificial leg.

I approached the bar, planted my right foot, and threw my body into the air, arching my back more than I had ever done before. My head cleared the bar, my hips got over but my left leg – the artificial one – came in contact with it. The bar shook and it wobbled but it stayed up. Success. The height was five feet, one inch, which was one inch over my head.

Each of the other two jumpers missed on his final attempt and I was given the red ribbon for first place.

When I got off the school bus that day, my dad was already home from work. I don't remember if I had to tell him or if he just saw that ribbon pinned to my clothes. I do remember that he was utterly elated.

My dad played a big part in winning that ribbon because we had something in our backyard that very few other kids would ever have. It didn't look like much. A bunch of old sofa cushions and bed mattresses, a bamboo pole, and two steel posts that we nailed into the ground. Most of the items were other people's trash but together – for me – it was a treasure. I think I was the only kid with a high jump pit in his backyard.

As a father of eight children my dad could not provide brand-new hockey equipment or store-bought bicycles. But what he did provide was even better. Time, energy, and ingenuity. I remember looking out the kitchen window seeing him in his green parka with a water hose in his hand making a hockey rink in the dead of winter. I remember seeing my bicycle turned upside down in his workshop as he worked for hours to fix the tire, grease the bearings, straighten the handlebars, and tighten the spokes. It might not have been brand-new but it ran like it was.

My dad helped me get over the bar to win that red ribbon. That was the day in Grade 8 when I started to dream that maybe, just maybe, I could have a career as an athlete.

ROB SNOEK is a sprinter and long jumper who represented Canada at three Paralympic Games – Barcelona, 1992, Atlanta, 1996, and Sydney, 2000. He was a silver and bronze medallist at the Paralympic World Championships in Birmingham, 1998.

KATE PACE LINDSAY

When you grow up in a family of ten children, you learn how to compete for just about everything. Whether it is running, eating, or putting on your pajamas, you learn to do it fast. Competition was not something we did; it was how we lived.

As kids we rarely sat still. My mother always wanted us "out of the house," so we played baseball, kickball, basketball, and volleyball in the summer, and we skated, went sliding, and skied throughout the winter. We got involved in sports simply because we loved it. We did not have goals of being "the best," we were just playing. We did not know much about things like the Olympics, or the World Championships, but in time we would learn. I loved my childhood.

I can remember the time I first heard the word "Olympics." I was in our family room. In the corner were a few glass shelves, backed with a long mirror. These shelves held our family's prized possessions, trophies. We would often stare up at the glitter and dream of one day placing a trophy of our own on the prestigious shelf. One day that dream came true for me and two of my brothers. We were ski racing in the Nancy Greene Ski League and our team took top spot. We marched proudly into that room and made our way to the back corner, pushed back the existing hardware, and made room for the newest set of trophies. We felt like we had arrived. We were Champions.

It wasn't until some time later that we asked, "What is a 'Nancy Greene,' anyway?" My parents had a book on the triumphs of Canada's most famous skier, Nancy Greene.

"Is she a real person?" we asked.

"Of course she is. She won two medals in the Olympic Games." We looked at the pictures in the book and saw this real person, Nancy Greene. She had won *two* trophies in her league called the "Olympics." Later, I picked up the book and began to take a closer look at this famous girl. The pictures were interesting, the medals so bright, but it was her sweater that caught my eye. I had been skiing for a few years now, but I had never seen a ski sweater like that. It was brilliant red with little maple leafs up and down each arm. That sweater was given to her in this "place" called the Olympics. I wanted to go to that "place" but more importantly, I wanted a sweater just like Nancy Greene's.

What I realize now is that a seed was planted in my heart that day to go to the Olympic Games and wear the Maple Leaf sweater on my back. It started very innocently, but the power of that vision was what took me to the top of my sport and to two Olympic Games. I began to understand that only Canadian Team members wear the Maple Leaf and I was determined to be one of them.

After being named to the Canadian Team, the dream expanded, to wanting to be the best on that team, to wanting to be the best in the world. On February 11, 1993, I was crowned the best in the world when I won the World Alpine Ski Championships.

There were many times throughout my career when I struggled and my goals were not met, when I did not stand on the podium to receive a trophy. It was in those times that I would bring myself back to the little trophy shelf and remember how I felt when I only had one on that shelf. My father would always remind me that it was supposed to be fun. And it was. I had accomplished my goal. I have worn the Maple Leaf sweater.

KATE PACE LINDSAY was a member of Canada's Alpine Ski Team in the Olympic Winter Games in Lillehammer, 1994, and Nagano, 1998.

LISA ALEXANDER

In 1996, the only synchronized swimming event at the Olympic Games was the team event – eight women in the water at the same time.

We decided to bring our team together for the entire season heading in to the Games. We had never done this before but we knew that to compete for the gold medal, we had to change the way we trained. Normally we swam with individual club teams across Canada and did not come together until four or five weeks before the international competitive season; we would choose a top routine developed by one of the clubs, learn it, make some minor changes, and head out to competition. This would be our first chance as a team from across Canada to develop a routine from scratch. It was exciting, but also incredibly challenging – we all had different styles, we had a history of competing against each other domestically, and each of us was used to having a big say and getting our own way with our club teams.

We all moved to Edmonton in the fall of '95 and started to work on our Olympic routine. It did not go well. We seemed to lack a clear vision of what it should be. In December the top Canadian judges confirmed our worst fears. Our team did not have what it takes to compete at the Olympic level.

With only six weeks to go before our only scheduled competition and seven months before the Olympics, we had to make a call: push on and try to make it work or start something completely new. We decided to take a risk and start over.

Music was the first decision, and a version of women singing "O Canada" kept playing in our heads. The new idea was born. We had an entire piece of music written for us by the Canadian group Psychic Mambo based on the melody of "O Canada." Unity would be the theme of our new routine. It was a perfect choice. It stood for the unity of our team, the unity of our country (we had just been through the national referendum in the fall), and world harmony. We were all passionate about the selection. If we were out there doing something we loved, we believed others would feel the passion and be swept up in what we were doing.

Months later, at the Olympics in Atlanta I remember walking out to swim with the mental image we all agreed on – open hearts glowing for all the audience to see. For me our performance was magical.

As our flag rose in second place beside the Stars and Stripes, I experienced a moment of immense pride. We had come together as a team, we had taken a chance, and we had conveyed our passion and love for our country through our sport. And we had won a silver medal.

LISA ALEXANDER was an Olympic silver medallist with Canada's Synchronized Swimming Team at the Olympic Games in Atlanta, 1996. She won three silver medals at the World Championships in 1995.

LEAH PELLS

In 1996 at the Atlanta Olympics I was fourth in the women's 1,500 metres, running my best time ever. When I got home, to my surprise, I received hundreds of cards, letters, bouquets of flowers and gifts. I was overwhelmed by the show of support.

In 2000, at the Sydney Olympics, I experienced support of a different kind. I had broken the talus bone in my foot prior to my heat yet still tried to compete despite the pain. I had to pull out after 30 metres. I sat on the infield and cried, feeling I had let myself and my country down.

When I got home, I could not believe the love and support I received *again*. People showed me that their pride in a Canadian athlete was constant. No matter how well I did or did not do, people were supporting me. I needed to know that it was not about winning, but about giving it your best. That is what sport is all about and that is what Canadians everywhere taught me.

LEAH PELLS was a member of the Canadian Olympic Team, Track and Field, at the Olympic Games in Barcelona, 1992, Atlanta, 1996, and Sydney, 2000.

MARGIE SCHUETT

The time was 1998. The place was Kuala Lumpur, Malaysia. Canada had participated in the XVI Commonwealth Games, arguably the most successful Commonwealth Games ever staged. By all accounts, these Games would serve as a measure by which all future Commonwealth Games would be compared. Being the Chef de Mission of Team Canada had in itself been an incredible honour that came after my partic-ipation in all levels of amateur sport in Canada for over 30 years. It truly was my proudest moment and certainly one that would provide me with more great memories than one deserves to have. However, it was the morning after the closing ceremonies that best defines my pride in being a Canadian and best explains the passion I have, both as a citizen and as a sportsperson, for Canadian amateur athletes.

As I awoke on the usual hot and sunny day that had greeted us for the entire month we were in Kuala Lumpur, I had an unusual feeling. Since it was the day after the closing ceremonies, everything should be winding down. There would be no competition jitters or possibility of crisis looming ahead, so I should feel terrific. Canada had competed well and there had been no major injuries or problems. Why would I have this uneasy feeling? I walked over to the window to begin my morning stretches and realized at once what had been gnawing at me.

I looked out to the courtyard separating the building housing the Canadians and a couple of other countries from the building across the courtyard housing the members of a large delegation from another country. In this courtyard lay the remains of what was I am sure every piece of paper available, garbage bags that had operated as water bombs and had now been diffused by the power of hitting the ground from over 15 floors up, fire extinguishers, and, yes, a piece of furniture or two broken into as many pieces as you could imagine. It was a mess.

I closed my eyes, thinking, "I hope no one was hurt," and then realized I would have been contacted if anyone had been injured. My astonishment became even greater as I realized I had slept through what looked like the results of a hurricane. I dressed quickly and headed for the door. I sensed an air of sheepishness from everyone as I passed through the hallways. I entered the main office and found everyone hard at work trying to clean up the files to prepare for our departure to Canada the next day. As I watched people running around, I noticed that one person had quietly picked up a large green garbage bag and proceeded outside to the courtyard. As she went, I could see others taking note, not wanting to say anything, but realizing that something was going to happen. People began to gather at the windows to watch. From both buildings you could see faces peering out at this lonely figure as she attempted to pick up and remove the mounds of garbage and remnants of the "celebration" that had occurred the night before. The different countries' elite athletes, coaches, managers, and staff stood and watched as this one Canadian began to attack the shameful remnants of the night before. There was absolute quiet. No one spoke. Not a word.

Suddenly, with subtle and magnificent silence, the lone Canadian dressed in red and white was joined by a fellow Canadian. And then another. And another. Suddenly, quietly, without a word being spoken, one person after another walked into the courtyard, picked up a garbage bag, and began the tedious task of cleaning up the mess.

As this ensued, it became apparent that the only people who were cleaning up were dressed in Canadian team uniforms. Other countries watched. Some observers drank coffee. Some chatted quietly among themselves as they watched. As Malaysian workers attempted to join in, the leader of the Canadian Team asked them to please wait while the mess was cleaned. It should not fall on them to clean up after those who had enjoyed the hospitality of their country.

After an hour or two had passed, the courtyard had returned to normal. It was neat and tidy with bundles of garbage made ready to be taken away. As the Canadian team members finished, the members of other countries' teams, the Malaysians, and numerous other bystanders who had joined the silent vigil began to applaud. The sound rose to a level that brought tears to my eyes. From a distance I heard someone cheer "Way to go, Canada!"

The pride shared at that moment by all those who participated in the clean-up was better than all of them winning a gold medal. At that moment there was an undeclared statement of what they were, where they came from, and what they value. Being a member of the "clean team" was a defining moment and made me realize that helping in whatever way I could to assist these wonderful young men and women in the pursuit of their dreams was an honour and privilege.

In a time when excellence is often assumed rather than earned, it is refreshing to see a group of people who range in age and interest come together as a team and pull together to do the right thing. I had often seen this capacity on the field of competition but seeing it now on the playing field of life made me even prouder to be part of this team.

MARGIE SCHUETT was Canada's Chef de Mission at the XVI Commonwealth Games, in Kuala Lumpur, 1998. She has competed in swimming, diving, and badminton.

ACKNOWLEDGEMENTS

We want to thank all of the athletes who submitted stories for sharing their personal moments of triumph and despair and for teaching us all so much.

We would like to thank Rick Minch for kindly and graciously facilitating our contact with the Great One. And an enormous thank you to Wayne Gretzky, an international sport icon and a Canadian legend, on and off the ice, for providing the foreword and reminding us that "winning isn't always about getting the gold. . . ."

FROM ROBIN MEDNICK

This book could not have been published without the insight, wisdom, and guidance of so many people. The athletes in Sydney who wrote letters to my son were the inspiration. The advice they wrote made me think beyond the moment and I dared to dream that one day we could share their incredible stories with the world.

David Crombie, Chair of the Toronto 2008 Olympic Bid, embraced this project wholeheartedly and his genuine enthusiasm and knowledgeable advice spurred me on. John Bitove, President and CEO of the Toronto 2008 Olympic Bid, and the entire Bid staff were unanimous in their support and encouraged me every step of the way. The late Carol Anne Letheren, CEO of the Canadian Olympic Association and IOC member, was excited to endorse this project and offered to help in any way possible. In particular I want to express my thanks to: John Bitove for saying the words "I love it! Go for it!" and supporting me in this endeavour; Carolyn Taylor for listening so often with an open heart when I needed another opinion; Karen Pitre for offering to do anything I asked; Angela Trunfio for her wise and understanding counsel throughout; John Wilkinson for opening doors and doing the legal work in his expert and considerate way; Phyllis Berck for her thoughtfulness and tremendous assistance in contacting athletes who were difficult to locate; Rhonda Cohen for her insight and superb knowledge of words; Jeff Evenson for his keen mind and intuition; Sarah Eyton for her great wit and plethora of clever ideas; Ana Kirkham for her moral support and steadfast conviction that this book would come to pass; Lisa Ohata for her quiet reassurance; Susan Adach and Elaine Collicott for their honesty and objectivity; Adrian Montgomery and Bob Stellick for their special efforts and assistance; Ken Martin for being the king of the database; Nicole Rioux for her understanding and compassion; and Kelly Gianopoulos, Andrea Gagliardi, and Jamie Michaels for their generous help behind the scenes.

There were so many others whose input was integral to this book: the "Wiseguy" committee for jumping on board when the idea was nothing more than that and for gently guiding the book through its labour and birth; Diane Ratnik for her enthusiastic assistance; Marnie McBean for showing me that the seemingly impossible is attainable and for so expertly crafting the questions that helped elicit the stories and memories we sought; the 25 "Team Captains" for persevering in collecting the stories within one month, by any means possible; the volunteers for phoning the Team Captains; Therese Roberts for volunteering to help with the administration for the "one" month that turned into four and for being my incredibly efficient and invaluable right hand throughout; Terry Leibel for sharing her thoughts and offering helpful suggestions; Naomi Kirshenbaum for her valued opinion and guidance; Barbara and Jeffrey Fineberg for helping to fine-tune my thoughts; Harvey, Zelda, Michael, and Danny Goodman for keeping their door open and listening so often; Gladys Shibley Mitchell for her silent direction and guiding hand; and Margaret Mitchell for her genuine advice and concern.

I loved working with my editors and publishers. Wendy Thomas, my talented and astute co-editor, was so successful in maintaining the essence and heart of each piece. I thank her for the warmth she always displayed and for making the wonderful homemade soups that we ate as we laughed and cried our way through the stories. Doug Gibson, Jonathan Webb, and Alex Schultz at McClelland & Stewart believed from the beginning that athletes had stories worth telling and gave me the freedom to share this vision. They were such a joy to work with!

This book would not have come about without the love and support of my family. Sol and Marni Mednick, Rosalie and Evelyn Nepom, Michael and Ruth Henry, and Daniel Henry and JoAnn Kurtz were staunch supporters throughout. Sam, my daughter, helped in collecting the stories and together with my sons, Milton, Mordy, and Zale, listened to me talk endlessly about them, offering advice, encouragement, and hugs whenever needed. My husband, Ed, shared all my ups and downs and never wavered in his love, support, and belief in me. My parents, Bernice and Milton Henry, opened a world of possibilities for me and after the early death of my father, my mother continued to give me the foundation to fulfil my dreams.

FROM WENDY THOMAS

Thanks to Jonathan Webb for giving me the opportunity to work on a book that I thought couldn't be done in the time available. And a huge thanks to Robin Mednick, who was instrumental in proving me wrong. She has amazing drive and determination, but above all, a great ability to motivate and, even better, to laugh.

INDEX OF CONTRIBUTORS

Adams, Jeff, 51

Alexander, Lisa, 230

Antoft, Susan, 26

Armstrong, Maxine, 140

Bernier, Sylvie, 138

Bettauer, Robert, 72

Bigras, Sylvie, 20

Bornemann, Rebeccah, 103

Boucher, Gaetan, 111

Brant, Rick, 193

Buday, Tamas, Jr., 188

Buday, Tamas, Sr., 183

Burka, Sylvia, 81

Cain, Larry, 202

Cannarella, Frank, 134

Carter-Smith, Cecelia, 50

Carver-Dias, Claire, 113

Chase, Jessica, 149

Child, John, 41

Clarke, Norman, 128

Clarke, Stephen, 143

Crooks, Charmaine, 212

Crothers, Bill, 98

Cuthbert, Linda, 173

Denys, Alec J., 79

Despatie, Alexandre, 66

Donnelly, Sharon, 124

Dunnett, Adrianne, 174

Ferguson, Tracey, 18

Finlay, Robert, 175

Flemmer, Carrie, 119
Fonseca, Peter, 210
Ford, David, 189
Fréchette, Sylvie, 198

Gill, Nicolas, 66
Goyette, Danielle, 36
Gross, George, Jr., 163
Groves, Kristina, 27
Guilbert, Alain, 86

Harnett, Curt, 14
Hatelt, Lorene, 136
Heese, Mark, 41
Henderson, Paul, 150
Hibbert, Curtis, 82
Holden, Jody, 159
Holloway, Sue, 167
Hood, Graham, 115

Iarusci, Robert, 190
Igali, Daniel, 76
Igorov, Metodi, 71

Jarvis, Patrick, 116
Joseph, Curtis, 73

Karrys, George, 221
Kavelaars, Monique, 95
Kidd, Bruce, 6

Killingbeck, Molly, 208
Kwasnycia, Don, 137

LaRoche, Philippe, 46
Laumann, Silken, 21
Lenarduzzi, Bob, 172
Levy, Sandra, 54
Lewis, Ray, 1
Ling, Lisa, 84
Longstaff, Moorea, 154

McBean, Marnie, 151
McCaig, Sandra, 222
McClellan, Reg, 9
Malowney, Margo, 160
Maurice, Pauline, 158
Morel, Sylvie, 39
Morris, Alwyn, 74

Ng, Joe, 57

O'Donnell, Dave, 40
Olmsted, Nancy, 147

Pace Lindsay, Kate, 227
Pells, Leah, 231
Pracht, Eva-Maria, 106
Przybyszewski, John, 24

Ransom, James, 139

Raphaël, Fabienne, 34

Ratnik, Diane, 99

Redden, Chrissy, 59

Reid, Pat, 108

Robinson, Jennifer, 45

Rolland, Nadine, 130

Roy, Aldo, 131

Rusnov, Rob, 48

Sandor, Akos, 30

Sawkiw, Warren, 182

Schuett, Margie, 232

Simmons, Mark, 31

Snoek, Rob, 224

Soellner, Ian, 197

St-Louis, France, 129

Strange, Michael, 13

Tanner, Elaine, 192

Tewksbury, Mark, 100

Thompson, Dan, 155

Tiessen, Jeff, 122

Trayling, Bill, 214

Tuck, Gord, 107

Tygesen, Tanya, 62

Visser, Guido, 86

Waldo, Carolyn, 65

Watson, Dawn, 64

Whitfield, Simon, 170

Wickenheiser, Hayley, 83

Wightman, Chris, 88

Wilkes, Debbi, 87

Winter, Victoria, 179

Worrall, James, 3

Young, Hilda, 5

ROBIN MEDNICK
was Coordinator for Team 2008, the athlete ambassadors for the Toronto 2008 Olympic Bid. She has been a dedicated advocate and volunteer in many community organizations. She lives in Toronto.

WENDY THOMAS
is a freelance writer and editor. She is the author of several gardening books and editor of the children's book *A Farley Mowat Reader*. She lives in Toronto.